Edited by: Kristi Kinsey
Cover Art and Photography: Trey T. Kinsey

Dedication

This book is dedicated first and foremost to the author of my life, Our Father in Heaven. His patience and wisdom have brought me to the point where I can write this book. As well, this work is dedicated to my bride, Kristi, who supports me no matter the crazy idea, this book is for you. I am so grateful to you for all the years of work alongside me, helping ensure the success of our ministry, and helping me craft the systems in this book. Thank you for the hours I spent writing this and not being with you. Thank you for being my greatest support and for not laughing at me when I told you I was going to write a book all those years ago.

Table of Contents

Introduction

I was twenty something once. After several rough years of turmoil in my life, I was searching for direction, purpose, and success when I finally began to understand a calling for ministry that I had honestly felt since high school but had run from. I had been a modern-day Jonah. Mostly because I grew up in a traditional Baptist church and my only frame of reference for being a worship leader vocationally (professionally) was that of a traditional music minister. While I have a deep love for this spiritual heritage, I had no desire to devote the rest of my life to this approach to ministry and worship and honestly felt no sense of peace about it either. So, I ignored my call for many years until I found myself leading a small worship band for a traditional Baptist church that was experimenting with an "alternative" service on Sunday nights. The hope was to attract younger working singles in the Jacksonville, FL area. I had been placed largely in charge of the service by the senior pastor, mostly because the music minister in place at the time didn't support our contemporary approach to the service. The service was a wonderful experience but met with some resistance in the church; although there was some support as well. Most notably missing from the support camp was the actual senior pastor after a couple months, the same guy who had asked me to lead the service a few months prior. During this time, I met and collaborated with another pastor who was consulting with our church while he was between church ministry positions. He later would launch a new non-denominational church in the area. I got a call from him one day and was offered a part-time position with the new church to come and be the worship leader and take over the small worship team in place. The previous worship leader refused to take off his hat during worship and was let go. He struggled to bury his own ego and so the worship leader role was open. Even in the moment I knew God was at work in my life as my path was becoming clearer and my calling to vocational ministry was coming into sharp focus. I was so excited.

I was miserably unprepared. At this point, I had been leading contemporary worship and worship teams since early high school. We had a high school worship team at my traditional church growing up and I was given leadership of the group my sophomore year. I'd also been involved in just about every other kind of church music group you can imagine. Everything from handbell choir, boys' choir, a youth choir that toured each summer, orchestra, you name it I've probably done it. I was also changing course with my college education and was starting a ministry education but had only just begun. My education, however, was not going to be of any help for years to come. I was taking over a "barely on its feet" worship team with the new church and I was excited that I would be able to lead this team how I wanted. I imagined having full control of things like rehearsal and song selections, leading awesome people who were always present, on time, and prepared. The non-denominational church was in full support of contemporary worship, and I was on deck to hit a home run.

Then ministry set in. I thought the years of worship leadership experience as a young man and a volunteer in churches up to this point would carry me through anything I would face. I was young and eager and experienced, and I was confident that would be enough. All that experience was good, but there was a lot I was missing. There were challenges I would face in the next few years that I was unprepared for. There are just some realities of significant ministry leadership and vocational ministry that are a whole different matter, even more so in worship ministry. Things you only glean with a lot more in-depth experience. There were tidbits of insight someone, somewhere could have told me which would have saved me a lot of headache and heartache. I wish someone would have handed me a resource with battled tested strategies for leading a worship team. I wish someone would have helped me with skills that had nothing to do with picking up my guitar and standing on the platform.

When I first had the prompting that I had something to share when it came to leading worship ministries, I had no idea what that meant or who would even listen. I spent almost a year arguing with God. I argued with Him about even writing this project. I argued with God that I had no credibility. At the time I felt led to write this book I was in between jobs with an actual church. I was still serving in a worship ministry but certainly not in a role with any clout or acclaim. I argued with Him that I didn't have the knowledge or authority to publish anything or write an entire book. God consistently showed me how small and foolish my arguments were. In the end, the Holy Spirit didn't drop the issue with me so here we are.

As with most situations where God asks us to do something we don't want to do or don't understand, the answers as to "why" come after we submit to God's will. For me, the "why" came only after the first time I sat with my iPad to put my thoughts together for this book. Only then did God give me the clear focus for this book.

My calling, my aim, and my hope for this book is to speak to young or first-time worship leaders who have recently assumed leadership of a worship team or worship ministry. Recently could mean anything really but basically there is a season as a worship leader where the best work one can do is learn, because you probably won't be doing much of anything else very well. Accept that you are "green" and new at this, don't stress or fret about it, move on, and decide for yourself to get better. Maybe "new" for you means a new job and you're looking to brush up your ministry skills. You'll be a better worship leader, pastor, colleague, employee, and friend if you do. Another selfish hope is that *anyone* who finds themselves in worship ministry will be able to read this and find at least something beneficial that they can incorporate into their worship ministry to make it better. I've been called to share what I've learned, and what I know to be true when it comes to leading dynamic teams of worship leaders in the local church. My dream is to help even one person who picks up this book. Even if you've been in worship ministry for decades, my prayer is that this book will be a tool to help you evaluate and improve your ministry and give you some new ideas. Your team and your congregation need you to constantly feed the fire of passion for your calling and your ministry and I hope this book can be another log on the pyre.

My goal is to impart some acquired wisdom, wisdom gleaned from over two decades of leading various worship teams and ministries in very different settings. I have been blessed in that I have found an approach to ministry and developed systems that have enabled me to have longevity in my career and not be one of those worship leaders whose tenure on average is typically less than three to four years in a single church. I have a unique perspective of having long stretches of service on only a couple church staffs for long, extended tenures while at the same time being exposed to many other ministries and their approaches and seeing the good and the bad in these other churches up close. I want to give you all the things no one gave me when I first started leading worship. I remember the stress, anxiety, and pain of learning the ropes of ministry, working with church people, and fighting the good fight in ways only experienced by worship leaders. Our experience of life devoted to ministry is a unique journey and we worship pastors and worship leaders seldom have deep pools of friends or colleagues that can relate to our struggles and encourage us through unique challenges. My sincere desire is to spare you some of the struggle I faced when I was first charged with ministry leadership and encourage you along the way.

Before we dive into the meat of this book, I want to make a promise to you, the reader. I hate reading leadership and ministry books that are full of fluff. My promise is to write a book that is full of practical solutions to the problems that we worship leaders face. As well, I understand you are busy and the time you take to read is sacred and precious. I promise to be concise and write a book that is to the point so you can get on with the other things you need or want to be doing. Know that there are many ways to go about conducting a worship ministry and there are many approaches and strategies. The ideas and systems I will lay down in this book are not perfect nor do I have all the answers by any stretch. But I have witnessed firsthand the effectiveness of many of these particular strategies for overseeing a worship ministry in multiple church settings. While there is always room for improvement and customization, these tips have led to team consistency and ministry health, and I wholeheartedly believe they could be useful and helpful for you if you are searching for ways to run a more effective ministry.

Worship leadership is not for the faint of heart and many times the things we are asked to do stretch us to the limits of creativity and drive. Sometimes we are asked to accept and perform the impractical, sometimes even the seemingly impossible, by senior pastors, congregations, worship team members, and even our families. I hope you can take away something from this book that will assist you in developing into a stellar worship leader that will rise to meet the challenges facing you as you begin or continue this exciting time in your life. Buckle up and hold on and enjoy this ride of being a worship leader. It is a privilege to serve our God and His people in this unique way, one that few people get the opportunity to live out.

THE LEAD WORSHIPPER'S HEART

1 – A Theology of Worship

"And so, dear brothers and sisters, I plead with you to give your bodies to God because of all he has done for you. Let them be a living and holy sacrifice—the kind he will find acceptable. This is truly the way to worship him. Don't copy the behavior and customs of this world, but let God transform you into a new person by changing the way you think. Then you will learn to know God's will for you, which is good and pleasing and perfect."

Romans 12:1-2 NLT

I'm going to make this section on theology really easy for you because I know you're thinking "I just want to know how to run a worship ministry, that's the only reason I am reading this book". I want to help you develop a theology of worship, however, because you need a foundation as to the purpose for your ministry role or vocation in the local church. Having a simple and clear worship theology will guide future decisions regarding vision and mission within the ministries that you oversee. This theological foundation is the basis for all the really meaty tips that you are seeking for your ministry. For you to really grasp why some of the systems I have utilized through the years work and work well, you must have a firm grip and passion for the theology that those systems rest upon. Certain choices in systems and strategies are successful because they are based on the eternal things that are most important in the life of the

Christian believer and rest upon the foundation of God's instruction found in His Holy Word.

So *you* should want you to have ownership of your theology. A theology that is fool proof. A theology that will enrich your life and challenge you every day to live a life worthy of the calling laid upon you. Are you ready for it? Do you want to know what it is? You sure? Ok, here it is; First of all, everything you need to know about worship can be found in the Bible! There it is. See how easy it is. You don't even *need* to read the rest of this book. Everything you could ever learn about for whom we worship and why we worship corporately and individually has already been written. I can't teach you anything "new" and I won't even try. I say this in the hope to implore you to, in all things that you do, keep a burning love for God's Word and *His* way of doing things. Coming up with it on your own will only cause you headache and heartache.

I can't say anything that hasn't already been said by God or one of His servants who helped pen the scriptures we treasure so much. What I can give you is the "Reader's Digest" version of what God has communicated about what He sees as proper worship towards Him. You may be young if you're reading this so let me explain a little about what Reader's Digest means.

Reader's Digest is a periodical publication that essentially made its fame as being a collection of short stories. Now these stories weren't just any tales or fiction. Most were true and factual accounts that told incredible stories of survival, love, and loss from all walks of life. The best thing about these stories is that they were brief. Reader's Digest was something you could pick up and put down regularly, frequently, but best of all briefly. Being a reader of Reader's Digest didn't involve a huge investment of time or attention. It was casual reading.

Now I don't mean to say that our reading of God's Word should be casual. What I intend is that for our purposes, our look at a theology of worship will be brief, approachable. Something you can pick up, put down, and come back to later. In this way, my hope is that you can develop a personal theology of worship that you can recall at a moment's notice. In no way can this examination be considered exhaustive but will hopefully provide some fundamentals for you to begin to develop a systematic worship theology. Eventually you will be faced with choices for worship services or environments or faced with defending your choices and having a strong theology of worship built into your decision-making process will give you a sturdy platform on which to stand when those times come. And trust me, they <u>will</u> come.

The Old Covenant - The Commandments of Worship

God's instructions on worship have never been singular, nor have they been fixed, but rather have simultaneously expanded and become more concise as He has continued to reveal Himself through mankind's history. We will begin with some instructions God gave to His chosen people, the Israelites, in the Old Testament. While those of us who are in Christ are not bound to the Old Covenant (law) anymore, these directives for worship give us great insight into the heart of the Father whom we serve.

First and foremost, God is jealous of our worship. This gets to the heart of for whom we worship. The first formalized instructions God gave to His set-aside people, the Israelites, began with instructions about a proper worship relationship with God. The time-tested and well known Ten Commandments begin with four commands that reflect how we are to demonstrate our worship.

The First Command boldly proclaims that the only acceptable worship is directed towards God only.

> 3 "You must not have any other god but me."
>
> Exodus 20:3
> *(New Living Translation, 1996/2015)*

God teaches us that He alone is worthy of praise and adoration. As sole creator, architect, and orchestrator of the universe, He alone deserves to have all of our devotion and love directed towards Him. Obsession and gratitude reflect our affection, and these should be directed to the one who sets our lives in motion.

The Second Command demonstrates the breadth of God's desire for us to worship Him and Him alone.

> 4 "You must not make for yourself an idol of any kind or an image of anything in the heavens or on the earth or in the sea. 5 You must not bow down to them or worship them, for I, the Lord your God, am a jealous God who will not tolerate your affection for any other gods. I lay the sins of the parents upon their children; the entire family is affected—even children in the third and fourth generations of those who reject me. 6 But I lavish unfailing love for a thousand generations on those who love me and obey my commands.
>
> Exodus 20:4-6
> *(New Living Translation, 1996/2015)*

While this passage is vivid and fairly self-evident, the key principle to understand is God's jealousy for our worship unleashes His capacity to abundantly bless those who love Him. Being obedient and offering praises to Him pleases God in such a way that He is compelled to love those who worship Him more deeply and more richly than we even have enough time to experience. It is for own our well-being by remaining in God's favor and love that we should seek to praise Him.

The Third Commandment pivots from directional worship, or vertically bringing pleasure to God, to heart condition. Every Commandment that follows after reflects the desire of God that our hearts be in right standing with Him and with others and that we might not be motivated by self-oriented thinking. This pivot will require a little more unpacking to fully grasp.

7 "You must not misuse the name of the Lord your God. The Lord will not let you go unpunished if you misuse his name.
Exodus 20:7
(New Living Translation, 1996/2015)

It is the deeply held belief of this author that words matter as much as actions do. Actions are the outpouring of one's heart, words are the window into the heart. Unfiltered words can be just as destructive or just as constructive, if not more than, actions we may take. The old saying goes "actions speak louder than words" but I believe words carry a bigger stick and can leave deeper wounds. One doesn't have to look far to see this principle at work in the bullying epidemic in our nation currently. Our young adults are driven to suicide because of constant words that degrade and destroy young egos. How many cases have you ever heard of some young person taking their life because they were physically harmed by someone else. I'm guessing not nearly as many. Physical harm is usually limited to infrequent occurrences. Bullying with words can carry on and on and go largely unnoticed. Proverbs even teaches that the tongue and it's power over our words carries with it the power of life and death (Proverbs 18:21). The above Third Commandment strikes at the heart of this reality of words.

To curse the name of God or to curse someone else using the name of God carries immense power in God's eyes. This truth must be self-evident otherwise why the commandment to not misuse the name of God or use the name in vain. The commandment is not to NOT use God's name but rather to be careful and cherish the power the name of God carries.

So how does this commandment relate to worship? As mentioned earlier, this commandment influences one's heart condition. God wants our love desperately and if we cannot cherish this important aspect of God, His name, how can we love and respect Him? This is similar to when we teach our kids that it is usually not acceptable to use adult's first names but rather they should appropriately use the names we have taught them such as Mom, Dad, Mommy, Father, Mr. or Mrs. Teaching our kids respect builds a foundation for love because our familial relationship is different, rather, something special. God wants to be God and wants us to be His people. Therefore, proper use of His name is the basis for respect and love. When we curse with the name of God or curse the name of God we not only disrespect our beloved God we also are tampering with spiritual power, the power of God's name. What kind of power? The kind that knocks armed guards to their backsides! (See the account of Jesus's arrest in Gethsemane in the Gospel of John Chapter 18)

In terms of being a worship leader, part of our job is to teach proper worship, of course, but I believe more important than that is helping our flocks fall in love with God. God is something special and He deserves to be cherished and is worthy of our love and worship. We must teach and model for our people the correct heart condition for proper worship and teach how our words reflect our heart condition. Our words matter, we must act like it and be passionate about teaching this truth to other disciples. God demands that His name hold a special place in our hearts and in our mouths.

The Fourth Commandment speaks to the importance of spending time with God and setting aside time in life to keep God first in our lives.

8 "Remember to observe the Sabbath day by keeping it holy. 9 You have six days each week for your ordinary work, 10 but the seventh day is a Sabbath day of rest dedicated to the Lord your God. On that day no one in your household may do any work. This includes you, your sons and daughters, your male and female servants, your livestock, and any foreigners living among you. 11 For in six days the Lord made the heavens, the earth, the sea, and everything in them; but on the seventh day he rested. That is why the Lord blessed the Sabbath day and set it apart as holy.

Exodus 20:8-11
*(New Living Translation,
1996/2015)*

God has asked us to take one day in seven and to rest in Him. God demonstrated His own preference for rest during creation and it is in the rest that we can intentionally take time away from our toiling and focus on being in God's presence thus keeping the day Holy. Being Holy is to be in God's midst. How can we love someone or something if we never spend time with them or spend time participating in some activity. Being a worship leader you probably know someone who struggles in their walk of faith and that struggle can be directly attributed to their inconsistent submission to the need for a sabbath. I don't think the command here is intended to be a command to *not* do other things (Jesus refutes this notion when the Pharisees attempt to trap Him with His words in Mark chapter 2), but rather a command to spend time with the one who is deserving of our time. Much like a husband and wife must be intentional about setting aside romantic time such as a "date night", we must be intentional in setting aside our days for the only purpose of being God's Holy people. While our worship can extend beyond this one day, God has given us a standard as the bare minimum time we should devote ourselves to worship and spending our time developing our relationship with our Creator.

The remainder of the well known Ten Commandments deal with our treatment of others. While they are no doubt important, the implication of these and other commandments found throughout the Old Testament scriptures can be best understood through the lens of Jesus's teaching on the Old Testament found in the New testament.

A New Old Commandment, or an Old New Commandment

Before we dive into the Reader's Digest deep-end of New Testament worship theology we need to base our examination on a couple assumptions to frame the discussion. For the purposes of this book we will assume that all aspects of New Testament worship are dependent on saved believers who have placed their faith in Jesus and have acknowledged Him as Savior and Lord. We will also assume the New Testament implores believers to gather together and therefore the collective, corporate gathering of believers for praise, prayer, and sharing of God's Word is an integral part of the New Testament church. As a worship leader I'm going to assume you've been a part of worship services and you know that we are called to gather together and that aspect of worship is required in church ministries that we may participate in.

In several of the New Testament Gospels (Matthew, Mark, Luke) Jesus is questioned as to which commandment is *the* greatest. Those asking are looking for the magic pill of honoring God. Their hope being that Jesus would give them a simple formula for following the *one* greatest commandment and somehow save them from the impossible task of keeping all of the hundreds of other commandments and corollaries found in the Old Testament Law. Jesus's answer is both the simplified solution they were looking for but also the culmination of what all the various laws and commandments were striving to achieve, thus honoring and not contradicting God's Word. If we as worshippers seek to love our God as best we can then our aim should be to obey His commands and Jesus instructs us to achieve this aim in this way:

> 28 One of the teachers of religious law was standing there listening to the debate. He realized that Jesus had answered well, so he asked, "Of all the commandments, which is the most important?"
>
> 29 Jesus replied, "The most important commandment is this: 'Listen, O Israel! The Lord our God is the one and only Lord. 30 And you must love the Lord your God with

all your heart, all your soul, all your mind, and all your strength.' 31 The second is equally important: 'Love your neighbor as yourself.' No other commandment is greater than these."

32 The teacher of religious law replied, "Well said, Teacher. You have spoken the truth by saying that there is only one God and no other. 33 And I know it is important to love him with all my heart and all my understanding and all my strength, and to love my neighbor as myself. This is more important than to offer all of the burnt offerings and sacrifices required in the law."

34 Realizing how much the man understood, Jesus said to him, "You are not far from the Kingdom of God." And after that, no one dared to ask him any more questions.

Mark 12:28-34
(New Living Translation, 1996/2015)

All of God's desire of our worship is that we love Him utterly and completely and that we love all the people He has created more than we love even ourselves. God comes first but how we treat other people in this life is of immense importance to our God. As we are His special created, so is the person to our left and to our right. As a worship leader and as one who works in ministry you must always remember that people must come before everything else that demands your ministry attention. There will be a thousand things screaming for your focus but you must remember that as you praise God, you must prioritize people above stuff. We'll look at this idea more later as we look at some practical ministry skills that will help you maintain this principle. You must be prepared to model to your ministry team and to your congregation that loving people is a commandment and true worship and love of God equates to true love of people. This means going the second mile for others. This means championing the belief that people are God's creatures and as such are worthy of love. Our love should seek to rescue, restore, and lift up people even when they act in ways undeserving of this love. As lead worshippers we must demonstrate following these commands and teach others to do the same. As Paul teaches in 1 Corinthians 13, we can do amazing things but without love, amazing deeds are pretty much useless and obnoxious noise in the eyes of God. You may have all the talent in the world on the platform but if it is all about you and your ego, you will run people over and cast people aside, people God has sent to you to minister to and disciple. In God's church, your people come before your music, your production, your gear, and your fame, always.

Lifestyle Worship

To this point, we have largely looked at a theology that is primarily Old Testament based. While there is much to be found on God's instructions for worship in the Old Testament, basing our expression of worship only on these instructions would leave our worship feeling rigid, programmed, and robotic. Jesus's life, ministry, crucifixion, and resurrection provided for us a radical new access to relationship with the Father. A way has been provided for us to move from being merely the created to being adopted members of God's family and co-heirs to His kingdom (Romans 8). Worship after the coming and ministry of Christ is distinctly marked by intimate relationship and as such our practice of worship needed to change. In the Old Testament, worship consisted of seeking to not break the rules God laid out in order that His people could be found blameless enough for God to dwell among His people. This dwelling still had restrictions, limits, and barriers. The tabernacle and the temple descriptions found in Old Testament scriptures reveal the restricted nature of the relationship we had with God. Only certain people could enter where God dwelled and only on certain occasions and with great limitation. After the salvation found in Jesus, we had unlimited access to the presence of God without having to lift a finger. We didn't deserve it and we didn't earn it. We were given a gift that brought us back to living with the Father, as we did in the Garden of Eden before sin entered the world. Every moment of every day we find ourselves in the presence of the Holy One without separation and we are now called to live lives worthy of this special intimacy. In Paul's letter to the Romans we see this new expression of worship and the implication for the Christ follower:

1 And so, dear brothers and sisters, I plead with you to give your bodies to God because of all he has done for you. Let them be a living and holy sacrifice—the kind he will find acceptable. This is truly the way to worship him. 2 Don't copy the behavior and customs of this world, but let God transform you into a new person by changing the way you think. Then you will learn to know God's will for you, which is good and pleasing and perfect.

Romans 12:1-2
(New Living Translation, 1996/2015)

This is no longer worship merely to check off the boxes of obedience and absolution of sins. Rather this is worship that seeks to honor the great gift of mercy from judgement of sins by living a life where everything we do or say glorifies God. Not because we are compelled to, but because we are so in love with our God. This is lifestyle worship. This is how we carry on a relationship with the Father. When we live a lifestyle of worship we are in a tighter relationship with our heavenly Father and that bond allows us to have more intimate knowledge of the design God has for our life. This knowledge allows us to be blessed and to find peace because we are fitting perfectly into the mold God has designed for us.

Lifestyle worship affects everything. From the moment we wake up we are to be praising the Lord through every word and deed. Paul's instruction is that even our bodies are not our own and are meant for worship. The implication of this aspect of worship affects our physical decisions, our spiritual decisions, and our emotional decisions. It impacts our world-view and our relationships. What we do with our entire being is our worship. Every decision, every reaction, every plan, and every thing we touch should be filtered through the objective of loving God, and loving His people. Simply showing up on Sundays (or whenever your church worships together) is no longer enough. Pursuing the goal of making ourselves like Christ should be carried out with an infectious intensity that glorifies God constantly, at every turn, and inspires others to follow the same path.

The *why* of this lifestyle of worship rests in holding up our end of the agreement of the New Covenant that Jesus instituted in the New Testament. At the last meal Jesus shared with his followers on the night before his arrest and crucifixion, he did something radical. He installs a new covenant, or contractual agreement, for the people of God. This account can be found in Luke's gospel (as well as other New Testament references). In this moment, Christ declares that we are free from being subject to the law of sin and that the church is subject to grace found in salvation through faith in Jesus. The moment is brief in the account in Luke's gospel but the implication alters human history. This access to grace means access to the Father in a new, uninhibited way. Being this close to our Father requires us to exist as expressions of worship. The sum of our total life should reflect our worship to the God who has saved us from sin and death merely because He chose to out of unspeakable love for us (Romans 6:23). We worship as praise, thanksgiving, and repentance for where we fall short.

This is the foundation for my worship teams. Nothing takes more importance than this discipleship principle. If I convey nothing else to my teams but this important reality of worship, then I still consider my efforts fruitful. Making the commitment to submit to this type of lifestyle is the next greatest step to living a sanctified Christian life after salvation and subsequent believer's baptism. This is really submitting to the Lordship of Jesus which requires growth and faith. This requires sacrificing self totally every minute of every day and requires constant, conscience effort. Any worship leader who hopes to lead a ministry and a church in worship of the Father must first be grounded in a lifestyle of worship. True and proper worship can't be manufactured once a week on a Sunday when it's time to get up and perform. Anointed worship leading flows out of a worship leader who has that tight bond with God that can only be achieved through the daily walk of lifestyle worship. And this principle applies to not only you as ministry leader but to your team members as well. If you want your worship team to achieve new heights in authenticity and zeal during your services, your discipleship efforts must begin with lifestyle worship. I discuss in future chapters how you can convey this message and build into your team's culture.

As well, as "lead worshipper" of your particular setting, you have a responsibility to assist the leadership of your church in conveying this aspect of worship to your entire church body. If we are to believe this is the greatest aspect of worship in the New Testament then it is not enough to believe it and live it by yourself. It is your job to model, promote, and teach this part of being a Christ-follower to everyone impacted by your servant-leadership. Your responsibility is to be the champion of this aspect of discipleship and to support your church's leadership team and whatever efforts help to move people along their spiritual journey to the place of lifestyle worship. Your local church may call this something different like being a full disciple, or being fully devoted, or even the high theological word of being *sanctified* but regardless of the nametag, you should be on the lookout for these efforts and find ways to reinforce the efforts through and within your ministry.

This theology of worship is by no means exhaustive. One could spend a lifetime alone exploring God's intention for His people and how we approach Him. One could spend another lifetime simply exploring the Psalms and its implications for our worship and I implore you to begin that exploration if you haven't already because this book won't be digging that deep. My hope, however, is that as you make choices and design the systems and strategies for your worship ministries that you now have a fundamental theology of worship for making strategic choices. Being able to defend *why* you want your people to participate in certain efforts or strategies will build your credibility as a leader but will also give you a firm, spiritual foundation as spiritual leader as you are tested in the waters of ministry. Your systematic theology of worship will no doubt look different from mine, but I firmly believe these to be the principles that must be the bedrock of any Christian beliefs on matters of worship. May this look at worship theology begin your study of worship that will take the rest of your life to complete! You are, after all, the worship leader, you should probably study worship regularly.

2 – The Role of the Worship Leader
in the Local Church

But among you it will be different. Whoever wants to be a leader among you must be your servant, and whoever wants to be first among you must be the slave of everyone else.

Mark 10:43-44 (NLT)

If you've just assumed the mantle of being worship leader in a local church, then you probably feel like you're in a line dance on a dance floor and don't know the steps. You know you fit in somewhere in the church structure but you're turning in circles just trying to follow the right order of things. You run the real danger of tripping over your own feet and if you're really bad off you may step on the toes of those around you. If you've been serving in a church for a while, you may have a better grasp on your role and your unique niche in the local church. Wherever you are, the reality is many worship pastors and leaders often don't have the proper idea of their role and this lack of understanding tends to lead to conflict. Conflict with the church, the staff, deacons, and worship team volunteers. If you want to have longevity in ministry, particularly within a single organization (anyone devoted to church unity should seek this), understanding how you fit into the scheme of things is required of anyone serving in the church. While conflict is sometimes unavoidable, there are realities I've learned that can help make sure that you are supporting your church and your fellow staff and adding value to your work environment. Trust me, you don't want to be the typical "worship leader". While your individual church's organizational or denominational structure may have an impact on your specific role, I have learned certain truths of how a worship leader should position himself or herself that can help ensure you add value to your organization and encourage everyone you come in contact with.

The Worship Leader is a Lead Servant, Not Lead Musician

There is no doubt that in the modern era, especially if you are in a contemporary setting, you will deal with a lot of music and the arts. Let's be real, you probably were given your role because of your musical talent on the platform. Your job is one of the few in the church where most of the benchmarks for getting hired are based on giftedness. Few churches are going to a hire worship leader who can't hold pitch or isn't proficient on an instrument suitable to leading a body of believers in song. And rightly so. The local church has hired you because they want to ensure that at the very least the person up front leading everyone else is appealing, attractive, and inspirational in musical qualities. Churches aren't in the business of scaring people off with terrible music; at least they shouldn't be. People may not stay because of good music, but they will certainly leave over bad music.

Here in lies the trap for us as worship leaders, however. Just because we got hired for talent doesn't mean we work *because* of talent. Your individual talent will only carry you so far and in my experience if that is all that you rely upon to keep your job, your ego that results from your talent will get the better of you in a number of potential ways and you won't keep your job, regardless of how talented you may be. Hear me when I say that I'm not advocating that you not care about your craft and pay no mind to developing as an artist. By all means, in most churches, the worship pastor or leader will likely be the most gifted artist around, but your role is so much more than showing up and making music. Being a worship leader bestows on you the privilege of influence that goes beyond showcasing artistic talent.

If you haven't heard or learned this lesson yet from your experiences, vocational ministry means giving your life to the mission of Jesus's Church. It is a life of sacrifice and submission. Really this is true of the entire Christian life but answering the call to vocational ministry means there is a mandate laid upon your life to carry this principal out. The local church is the local representation of the Kingdom of God and Jesus was quite clear how we are to orient ourselves in His church:

> "42 So Jesus called them together and said, 'You know that the rulers in this world lord it over their people, and officials flaunt their authority over those under them. 43 But among you it will be different. Whoever wants to be a leader among you must be your servant, 44 and whoever wants to be first among you must be the slave of everyone else. 45 For even the Son of Man came not to be served but to serve others and to give his life as a ransom for many.'"
>
> Mark 10:42-45
> (New Living Translation,
> 1996/2015)

It's clear that as you work and conduct ministry in the local church you will exert influence over others. Influence *is* leadership and leaders in Jesus's church are servants and slaves.

Being a great worship leader in the church means being one of the greatest servants to those *in* the church. Your leadership must be marked by sacrifice and deference to others so that you will accomplish great things for His glory. You will be required to set an example to the rest of the body. You must lay down your own dreams and goals and needs and take up those of your fellow pastors, elders, deacons, members, and seekers that you meet. Worship leaders who don't seek God's kingdom first stick out because our role is so visible on the platform. Our worship team members will also see right through us because they are the ones who spend the most time with us at countless rehearsals, sound-checks, and services. They see us when we are squeezed by sound glitches, deadlines, and challenging church members. These are the moments when you get to display what your true motivations are and what you deeply care about. If you want to destroy your worship team in a hurry, be all about you and you'll see how quickly people bail from your ministry.

Serve...

Particularly, be lead servant to your pastor. You have no idea the weight he carries and the sheer volume of work required to lead the local church as lead pastor. Old Testament scriptures tell of Moses praying and worshipping while a battle raged in front of him and while his arms were raised in worship the Israelites would surge and if he were to let them fall the Israelites would begin to be overwhelmed. The implication being that as Moses's posture of worship goes, so goes the battle. The story also tells of Aaron and others helping to keep Moses's arms raised. (Exodus 17 NLT) Are you helping your pastor wage war or are you acting like his enemy and making his working life difficult? When was the last time you helped raise your pastor's arms? When was the last time you prayed for him and asked God to encourage him? Have you recently asked how he's doing or offered to take over some task that weighs on him or would free him to do other things only the lead pastor can do? When he puts you in charge of something outside your regular duties do you thank him for the responsibility, or do you grumble? If we are to be lead servants then don't forget serving those in your immediate sphere like your colleagues and members of your deacon or elder board. A church marked by those serving one another in Christ's love is a church that will be a blessing to anyone who steps foot on campus.

This brings me to another matter that I implore you to grab onto and build into the culture of the ministries you oversee. *People come first; ministry matters come second.* As lead servant, you must keep lodged into your heart the burden that every interaction with a human being is an opportunity to serve, minister, witness, and encourage. It's really easy in ministry to get focused on and overwhelmed by the details of overseeing and implementing a ministry and fail to actually engage in any actual ministry. Auditions, technology glitches, and scheduling conflicts are always going to be blinking in your face and if you let them, they will blind you to the actual flesh and blood needs bubbling all around you. There will be times when you will find yourself in a dilemma of choosing between solving some A/V crisis and listening to someone who has had a garbage week. Choose now that you will choose the person. The impersonal matters will likely be there later, but the interpersonal opportunities can be missed in a heartbeat. Someone on your team or in your church body might not be willing to talk or divulge a need later and you run the risk of them thinking you're not concerned and never available. Your people need to know that no matter what they can have your ear, your heart, your hands, and your time. If you want devoted and committed team members and church attendees, be there for them even when everything is swirling around you in chaos. Realize this may affect quality and excellence levels sometimes, but remember you are a servant before anything else, and you can't be a servant without someone to serve. People come first; *stuff* comes second.

Being a lead servant also means elevating your worship team over yourself. One of the most important duties you have as worship leader is to equip and elevate the other servants around you on your worship team. If you find yourself singing every song, playing every intro, or shredding every guitar solo, you're likely on the wrong path. Please listen to this important reality; you have people all around you with incredible talent. Are they more talented than you? Maybe. Is that something to be afraid of? Absolutely not! God has given out talents to all kinds of folks and in all different ways. You have to be intentional about encouraging others to grow and utilize their talents and you have to actually let them use them. Give up the mic, play less, let others help plan. You serve others on your team by letting them contribute and have a stake in the ministry. Remember we are called to make disciples of the gospel, not back up singers. One key element of being a disciple is that eventually one's growth leads to the point where a person starts taking on ministry responsibilities. Your job is help people prepare for these responsibilities, not to be the barrier to their expression of God-given gifts.

Practically, you are best able to carry this out by having good ministry systems in place that help with planning and implementation which ultimately preserves excellence and keeps chaos to a minimum. We'll dive into these systems in future chapters and I highly encourage you to implement them into your ministry so that you are able to focus on mission instead of madness.

One other area you should realize that you are a servant is in the area of church resources. Modern worship experiences are expensive. Moving lights, video screens, digital audio consoles, keyboards, drums, and amps all cost big bucks to invest in and big(ger) bucks to maintain. Depending on your specific church, it will likely be part of your job to oversee the worship space and everything that goes into keeping it a blessing and not a curse to those who choose to come worship in your environment. This means being a good steward over resources. Hopefully I don't have to tell you about all the parables found in Jesus's teachings about the mismanagement of resources and gifts. Suffice is to say you will be trusted with resources that come from God's people being generous and you can best serve them by making wise and informed investments and cherishing the tools you have in place. I often tell my team to please take care of stuff like it belongs to their grandma, pretend its old and fragile and needs delicate hands. You should model and promote good stewardship among your ministry because you are serving the kingdom's needs.

As an artist it really can't be helped that you will find yourself the object of focus at times. Hey, you're talented, it's a gift from the Father, so celebrate! In order to lead, sometimes, it is necessary to have the eyes of your people on you. They can't follow if they aren't looking. You must, however, remain vigilant that as your music and art are attractive it should be for the purpose of pointing towards the Savior. Otherwise, you will fall victim to serving yourself which will only feed the ego monster. Let's kill him, shall wc?

3 – Burying Your Ego

He must become greater and greater, and I must become less and less. "He has come from above and is greater than anyone else. We are of the earth, and we speak of earthly things, but he has come from heaven and is greater than anyone else..."

John 3:30-31 (NLT)

If you've been in vocational ministry for a while you've probably realized that there are some stereotypes for the various pastoral or leadership roles that are common to most protestant evangelical churches. Most are light-hearted and honestly pretty funny. Did you know there is one called the "Worship Leader". These days you can pick them out almost exclusively by the skinny jeans. They're usually always late to meetings, have some facial hair, like to wear hats, and are generally flaky. I've heard it said that in every joke there is a measure of truth. Unfortunately, some of the aspects of the stereotype of worship pastors and worship leaders are not positive, and I don't think it's always undeserved. We're moody, we're egotistical, we're "artsy" which is just a (slightly) polite way of saying we're weird and socially awkward. We worship leaders tend to have similar personality traits because of the nature of our gifts and our calling and these traits can sometimes make it so that we don't play well with others. Being artistic carries with it a couple tendencies that if we fully allow to dominate who we are can make us particularly self-oriented.

First of all, artistic expression tends to make us really in touch with our emotions. The best artists, musicians included, have a gift for feeling something and creating empathy in others to feel the same thing through their art. This means exploring a lot of our emotions and a deep self-awareness of how we are feeling at any given time. This is a whole lot of time spent with one's self. Thinking about self, talking about self, writing, and singing about self. Sometimes this gets masked a little in worship music because we are able to direct self towards God, but we are still part of this equation. This much self-orientation can really lead us to places where we are far too concerned with our feelings, especially when we feel slighted or attacked. This much self-orientation is not attractive to a lot of people, and this is exaggerated when we're talking about Christ followers who view humility as a hallmark of being Christians. It is really important that you not let your ego take over how you interact with people. Let's be real, we worship leaders have to possess a lot of confidence in ourselves in order to step out and lead music and sing in front other people. There are people in this world who would be terrified if asked to do what we do on a weekly basis for our church services. But you must relate to others in humility and *then* lead in confidence. Dumping "you" and your emotional awareness on other people every time you're around will give you a reputation of being all about yourself, and that simply undermines your leadership in the local church.

Secondly, we get defensive of our talent. After long enough of being an artist you'll have people tell you you're good at something or have someone tell you they were really encouraged by something you did. This can be a great rush and make us feel good about ourselves. But how do you feel if someone is critical of your craft? What if someone wants to change something you've planned and practiced? Part of the stereotype of worship leaders is that they can be really inflexible. We feel a deep personal connection to our art and our worship services and this spills out when we think someone is trashing what we've put together. Sadly, this comes off not as passion but as ego. We have some vision in our heads for how a song should be played or what the volume level should be at. Without fail, someone will disagree with your choices or just not like your style of how you play keys. When these attacks come we run the danger of lashing out at the personal attack and this is because our ego is under assault. But what if your ministry wasn't based on ego? What if you worked and toiled and performed with purpose and calling, would you feel so insulted? Or would you rather feel secure, maybe even justified in your work because you've based your efforts on greater meaning than being a great musician.

A few years ago I came under very public assault from someone who had been attending my church. I initially met this individual when they came forward to sign up for our Worship Arts Team during one of our recruitment days (more on that in a future chapter). We'll call this guy Sam. Sam struck me as a really cool guy. Sam came to us via the Army moving his family into our community and he told me he had been a worship leader at a previous church in his past. He also told me he had some experience in Nashville recording with a band and traveling a bit. When we began Sam's audition process here at the church I was really impressed. Sam could really sing and really play. I really thought Sam was going to be a great addition to the team and would be one of the folks that could lead services and fill in for me when I was out of town. I had a real high impression of Sam. He really had talent and it seemed like he had a great heart condition to be a leader in the church. This is a point where some worship leaders might let their ego get the better of them and feel threatened, but I was genuinely excited about Sam.

Then Sam fell off the planet, poof! He was mid-way through our audition process and he just stopped showing up. Needless to say I was pretty bummed by it. Even after follow-up attempts of communication with Sam, I never heard back from him.

It was about a year later when Sam came back on my radar. I was just sitting down to lunch after church with my family and some church friends at our local favorite Mexican restaurant when I noticed I had a notification on my cellphone. The notification took me to Facebook where someone had left a review of the church on our public church Facebook page. It had been left by Sam and he had only given Liberty two out five stars. Two measly stars, that was it. The three blank stars were such an eye-sore to me. We tend to get positive reviews on these kinds of online forums. Well, being senior staff at the church, of course I'm concerned as to what had happened that would lead Sam, after a year of attending the church, to suddenly leave such a low rating. Opening the comments, I realize I see the words "worship leader" in the body of the text. Sam had great things to say about the church and our lead pastor but "the worship leader is like Chris Tomlin and that really ______." The blank wasn't a polite word. A term associated with the action a vacuum might perform. Sam's negative feelings and review of our church were aimed entirely at me and my likeness to Chris Tomlin. Can't say I'm a huge Tomlin fan but couldn't say I felt bad being compared to the guy, I mean he is a huge influence and an impactful worship leader, I might even venture to say anointed. But still, two stars because of me, because I'm too similar to Mr. Tomlin. The worst review rating ever left for the church on the Facebook page.

While it wasn't fun or uplifting to have that kind of attention, it genuinely only bothered me for about thirty seconds. My ministry is about so much more than me. There are dozens of folks contributing to our services that make them exceptional and I realized he was too focused on me, and he was missing everyone else. I didn't feel threatened or embarrassed because our Worship Arts Team is not about me, or anyone on our platform for that matter. We have a purpose that is fixated on our God and our people who attend. In the end, my team approached Sam on my behalf without my request to defend me and while I didn't need that it was nice to see the dividends of investing in others and the demonstration of loyalty that results from me putting my team above myself on a consistent basis. I was able to not allow this experience to shake me or make me feel threatened because I seek to constantly bury my ego. I make the ministry about something other than myself. Something other than my likeability or my talent. This helps me surrender the need to protect and defend myself and feel offended when my visible role is attacked. I chose to act in the church's best interest and Sam's best interest by not needing to engage in some conflict in order to defend myself and my reputation.

So how do we as leaders in the church get to the point where we can behave this way? How does an artist like a worship leader bury their ego when so much of their job is about performance and talent? This goes hand in hand with your role in the church as we discussed in the last chapter. Your role as a lead servant in the church will force you to make some cultural shifts in your ministry.

First of all, being a lead servant will require that you meet the needs of others above your own. This forces you to build your ministry and its systems around elevating and equipping others. When you are busy coaching others, celebrating the successes of your ministry, and troubleshooting the shortcomings of your accomplishments, you have a lot less time to worry about yourself. This also ensures you aren't in the spotlight non-stop. Elevating others requires that you share responsibility in worship. Others need the opportunities to sing lead parts or be the one who leads the entire service. Let others be the connective tissue that makes your services flow. Let others count in or play the intros. Make sure prayers and scripture readings are shared responsibilities. The people God has sent you to be on your team need to be able to express their gifts in God's church and you must serve their needs as people. They also need lots of instruction and encouragement as most of your people will likely be volunteers, not professional musicians, pastors, or church staff. Giving them that time and investment forces you to spend less time obsessing over yourself. You should be constantly searching for techniques and strategies to make your team better worship leaders. Help them be better singers. Agonize over them being better players. Celebrate when they grab ahold of the reigns of a service and usher people into God's throne room to worship. Giving away your job means you won't be getting all the attention and that's an awesome thing because it means you are succeeding at your real job of equipping others to be worship leaders.

Second, you must accept a reality that will likely never change over the course of your vocational ministry years. You, friend, are quite simply *replaceable*. Ouch that stings a little. The reality is no one else can do you, but there are plenty of other people that can do *what* you do. They might do it better, they might not. The truth is that as a worship leader or worship pastor you will always work for someone or something else. Depending on your environment, you either work for a lead pastor, an elder board, a denominational governing body, or some governing board. On any day your supervisor could wake up and decide it's time for a change in worship ministry. As well, the Lord can call you home at any time. How ever it happens there will come a time when someone else will be doing your job. Now I'm really not trying to scare you (well maybe just a little). Really, I'm trying to free you and encourage you. You have to accept that you being replaceable is a good thing. Do you really want the success or failure of God's church or even more specifically the worship ministry at your church to hinge on one person? Do you really want your ministry on such unstable footing that the removal of one person would cause it to crash and crumble to bits? Do you want to feel that way about one of your team members? That should make you feel really nervous and sick to your stomach. So why do you want your church feeling that way about you? They shouldn't and you shouldn't either. Your aim should be to build a ministry that would barely even notice your absence. You *want* to be replaceable. You are, after all, working for God's church, not your own success. When you accept this truth, your ego is truly being buried and then you can begin the work of being a blessing to your church and its people by being a leader that is instructed by God's vision for the church's future.

You also have to realize that you will get what you model. Ask yourself this question honestly, do you want a worship team full of self-centered, ego maniacs? If you're like me then that question should frighten you. Well guess what, your team is going to follow your lead. Now that's not to say everyone is going to be exactly like you and your personality. The truth here, however, is that you are your team's greatest champion for team culture. If your model is a leadership style and ministry systems that elevate you as leader and keep the spotlight aimed at you, then everyone is going to grab hold of the *me first* attitude. If you model sacrificial love and a servant's heart and posture and position yourself as someone who elevates and celebrates others, your ministry will undoubtedly be characterized by the same qualities. You will see in your team the traits you model and the behaviors you allow yourself to indulge in.

Now here's my warning, if you can't accept this, if you can't lay down yourself and put your ministry and its people first then you need to seriously pray about being in vocational worship ministry. If you can't be lead servant and not lead musician in the local church, then put together a band and cut an album and hit the road. You will find nothing but frustration and conflict on a regular basis if you can't be motivated by serving everyone else's needs before your own in the local church. You will not have thriving worship teams, you won't see growth in your people, your direct reports will turnover, and you'll find yourself a part of the statistic of short tenured worship leaders the church as a whole currently faces. But if your passion and your calling is to serve the Bride of Christ in a local church, then bury your ego now. Make the choice to be a great worship leader who cares more about discipleship than perfection of artistic expression and certainly more than self and let us get on to talking about how best to run the ministry. You should feel relieved knowing the church won't burn to the ground if you aren't around. In fact, let's celebrate that you are replaceable and start building a ministry that thrives in this truth. My hope is that the remainder of this book gives you some practical ways to build a worship ministry that is focused on worshipping the Lord and serving others both on your teams and in the church at large.

Section 2

THE LEAD WORSHIPPER'S TOOL BAG

4 – Opening the Door

---

*Now these are the gifts Christ gave to the church: the apostles,
the prophets, the evangelists, and the pastors and teachers.
Their responsibility is to equip God's people to do his work
and build up the church, the body of Christ.*

Ephesians 4:11-2 NLT

If you've just taken on the mantle of being worship leader for your church, it's an exciting time. There may or may not be history for your worship team, but either way you're probably excited to be in charge and start running things the way you'd like to see them run. If you've been running your ministry for a while, maybe you're looking for some new methods to conduct the ministry. Either way, there is one fundamental truth that is going to be a reality to running a worship ministry; you're going to be leading a team and you need people involved. Regardless of music style, or whether you're a real radical and you use moving lights in worship or not, you are not an island, and a healthy worship team needs participation from church members. This will be a challenge for the rest of your ministry years, you will always be short-handed and in need of more folks for scripture says "'…the harvest is great, but the workers are few!'" (Matthew 9:37 NLT). While God is ultimately in control of who He draws to your church there are some things you can do to help build the ranks of your worship team.

While there are many practical ways to recruit, the biggest thing you should always remember is that you need to find multiple ways to convey to your church family that the door is open for people to join your team. The reality is that when people are serving on your platform it looks full. Now *you* may wish you had three more or even thirty more people on your team but to the person sitting in the seats they see people and they usually assume the church has exactly what it wants in place. Other than the occasional brave, entrepreneurial soul who really wants to be a part of the worship ministry, unless you tell people there is room for them to join, they will simply assume there isn't room. One of your jobs leading a worship ministry is to create a culture that communicates the door is always open. Now the reality is as your quality improves in your worship experiences, that excellence level will attract quality people to your ministry team, but you can be more proactive than hoping people just show up on their own accord. Your approach should be multi-pronged to be effective, but the key is to communicate often that your team welcomes new people. You must engineer as many ways as possible in the life of your church to consistently communicate that your worship team isn't a clique, and that new people are always celebrated. So, let's look at a few ways you can go about letting people know that you're hunting for new team volunteers.

The Recruitment Day

This really is a big, glorified excuse to let people know the door is open. My team calls this the Worship Arts Team Reception. We do Reception once a school semester, usually a couple weeks into the semester once the church isn't promoting all its other back-to-school or new-year's programs. We promote the event two to three weeks ahead of time in both our electronic newsletter and from the platform either with a live announcement or a video promo. The idea is to let the church know that the worship team is looking for new folks to serve. Be intentional about letting people know you need musicians, production team, and creative types. We also typically highlight particular roles that we're dangerously short-handed such a bass guitarist or sound engineer, etc. We also make it a point to say something along the lines that the team is looking for all kinds of creative people and if they have a creative talent or skill to share to come on out and let us know. We've gotten everything from carpenters to knitters. We invite them to join us at the front of the worship platform after service on a scheduled service day. We have members of the team present to answer any questions they might have or give them a behind-the-scenes tour of our space and/or production booth. Ultimately, we're hoping for signups but sometimes people need to test drive something before they commit, and this is a good opportunity for them to look under the hood. Having other team members present does two things for you. One, it keeps you from being the only one able to answer questions or make connections. You can't be in two places at once so don't try. When we've done these events, we've captured anywhere from one recruit to twenty. Make sure you have other people around to be there to meet with new folks interested in the team. You can answer more questions about how the team operates when there are more folks available to field questions. The other thing having current team members present does for you is it adds credibility to the ministry. You can talk about how great your worship ministry is until you are blue in the face and still only come across as a used car salesman making a pitch. You're paid to say good things about being involved and people know it. But when your lay volunteers are there to vouch for the team it is much more attractive because they are able to be more authentic. It's the same feeling we get when we read good reviews about a product on Amazon. The item description sounds good but when a customer who bought the product vouches for it, we feel much better about committing to purchasing. The same is true for potential ministry volunteers. People want to know that the extra time they're investing in being involved in the ministry is worthwhile and having your people there tends to put people at greater ease.

We also have available sheets outlining the various roles available within the Worship Arts Team and it is broken down into Platform Team, Production Team, and Creative Team. This allows people to get an idea of whether they really are a fit. There may even be some way of serving on your team they hadn't even considered and now you've given them an outlet to serve in a new exciting way. Paired with these info sheets we have our church's Volunteer Application available. Your goal should be to get commitments on the spot. When people walk away without committing the statistical likelihood of them signing up later drops off a cliff. While not every sign-up pans out to be a committed volunteer, someone who doesn't sign up never turns into a volunteer. Yes, there are the occasional folks who need to take a serious look at their schedules and commitments to see if your ministry's schedule is doable, but I prefer to make the decision with them if I can. A lot of times folks assume things about how much time serving is going to take and I'd rather have their info and be able to chat with them about matters via email, or text, or even over the phone if they are hesitant to jump in. This can only be accomplished if you have their contact info. Having them go ahead and sign up also means you can begin your process for getting them connected to the ministry quickly. The process for getting people from sign up to serving on your platform can take time when you include things like auditions and training. The faster you can move people through that process the more they feel like they are actually wanted on the team. The more you drag this time out, the more people feel like they are more of a bother to you and may feel offended over the perceived exclusion.

There are other fun things you can do at a Recruitment Day to build excitement for being a part of your worship ministry. We ALWAYS do backstage tours. We are blessed with a really exceptional worship center and we have a great green room space. We also have a really cool Production Booth that looks flashy. We're no Hillsong or Bethel but we're proud of what God has allowed us to build for His glory. Giving people a behind the scenes look into your church can build excitement but can also build a relational connection with people who are "looking under the hood" of your ministry. It shows that it's not magic or even professionals making your church service work, it's church volunteers just like them. This can really help break down some resistance to serving because it helps remove a lot of the unknown and makes your ministry feel much more approachable. We've also done things like have food available, give out balloons or silly dollar store gifts, and pray with people as the need arises, after all its still a great opportunity to do ministry with folks face to face. If your church has some worship recordings this might be a great time to give a few copies out, too.

Our team feels like even if we only get one person to commit on a Recruitment Day, then it is worth the effort and investment to do the event. Again, your main purpose is to communicate consistently that the door is open to serving with your team. This is one of the most public and visible ways that you can tell people you're looking for them to join your team.

Volunteer Application

Hopefully your church is serious about people getting engaged and serving in a ministry somewhere in your church. If your church is like mine, its built into our discipleship process and we expect our people to be serving somewhere. As a part of our process, we have a Volunteer Application. This is where people can give us their contact information and their preferences on where they'd like to serve. We also have space for them to tell about any ministry experience they might have and there is a portion for them to give us the necessary information to run a background check as our church screens EVERYONE who even might be working with our kids.

It is essential that listed on the Volunteer Application are the available ways to serve on the worship team. You'd be surprised at how many churches assume talented folks will automatically find their way to the worship team. This just simply isn't true. By not having worship ministry listed on these types of forms it serves to only reinforce that the worship team is a closed group and newcomers aren't welcome.

Let me encourage you to make sure that people can sign up for your worship ministry on any of these types of documents at your church. Whether it's something available at your church's welcome desk or something handed out in a new member's class, the more avenues the better.

Also, don't worry about getting too detailed with what information you are seeking about your potential sign ups. This is especially true if your church's signup sheet is like our Volunteer Application which services all our church's signup needs. You may be tempted to try and get all sorts of information such as what instrument they play or what lighting consoles with which they're familiar, but I'd argue the application is not the best place to uncover this information. The best way to get that information is with a personal conversation. This allows you to make a first initial contact after they sign up in a personal way. This also ensures the first contact after signing up is about getting to know them more which helps you convey that you are generally interested in getting to know them and sincerely excited that they've decided to serve on your ministry team. These follow-up conversations need to take place within twenty-four hours of you receiving their sign up. These folks have stepped out on the limb to jump into something, and we should convey we are eager to have them on the team, eager to get them connected to other team members, and eager to begin the process of getting them ready to serve during worship services.

Church Website

Since we're living in the 21st century I am going to assume that your church has a website. I assist a lot with our church's web content and have done so for many years so I'm a bit of a student of church websites. I've seen even small churches with decent sites so for the sake of argument we'll assume your church's site is in place and at least functional. What I won't assume is that you are leveraging your church's webpage. While I'm a fan of simple webpages that aren't drowning in content on each page, I am a believer that each ministry of a church should have a way to highlight its values and programs. Most important is the ability to sign up for serving.

If you don't have a page for your Worship Ministry then that is something you can do today to start impacting the growth of your ministry. Realize that these kind of pages on a website are into the weeds of your church's website and you will likely be speaking to people who already attend your church and are looking for more information. Someone who is a potential church guest statistically is not likely to be on your site long enough to find their way to the Worship Ministry page, but it doesn't hurt to convey a few concise points about the culture of worship at your particular church. The main point of having a page for the worship ministry on your church's site is to allow another open door for people to get connected and start serving. You're not trying to convince people the church should have worship or even convince people of your church's style of worship. People that find this worship ministry page are already coming to your church, likely already bought into your approach. You are instead utilizing this page to expand your team.

I recommend right at the top having a clickable link that says something along the lines of "Signup To Serve With the Worship Arts Team!" and link it to your church's online volunteer application or at the very least an email or contact form where they can contact you directly or your church's assimilation pastor depending on your situation. Having this available and having content that speaks to the open-door nature of your ministry on the page aids in the multi-pronged approach to letting people know you're always looking for worship ministry volunteers.

Once your page is in place, then you can utilize the link for the page to constantly share the message that the door is open. Include it in your church's newsletter on regular basis. Send it to people who you've been told are musicians or good with computers. Include it in any marketing materials that go out that are related to Recruitment Days. No need for them to show up when they can go ahead and sign up online if they're interested and eager. The point is that you have a tool to constantly share the message that people are welcome on your worship team.

Holiday Programs

You're probably wondering how in the world can a holiday program possibly grow your team? If you're like me you're probably thinking about all the time and energy it takes to stage a Christmas or Easter program. You may even be thinking you don't feel capable of pulling off a holiday production if you're in a contemporary setting. Don't fret, you're in good company. I felt the same way some years ago. First of all, there are really great resources out there of pre-packed holiday programs that are specifically designed for modern praise worship teams. Moreover, even if you don't buy a resource like that, you are no doubt creative and you can put something together to celebrate the high times of worship on the Christian calendar. But all that aside, you should secondly consider that holiday programs are another great way to open the door to your ministry. My recommendation for holiday programs is that they typically require separate rehearsals. It's exceedingly difficult to stage a holiday production in the midst of on-going weekly worship rehearsals. To execute a holiday program with excellence it requires separate focus time to work on important aspects that make the production special. This reality, however, provides you with an opportunity to advertise to your local church that people are invited to be a part of the specific team involved with the program. The best part is that when people jump in and commit to the holiday program, they generally get a taste for worship ministry, and this makes the holiday program a gateway program for your on-going worship ministry. I like to inform those that have made it through our audition process or our production training program for our holiday program that they are automatically grandfathered into our worship ministry if they would like to continue on. The only step required is for them to sign our Worship Arts Team Covenant just like all our worship team members do (more on the covenant principle to come in a future chapter). I have found that nearly all holiday program recruits continue on to serve in our on-going worship team. While a holiday program is for the purpose of blessing the church and your community and sharing the gospel message of course, you can leverage the program to have an additional benefit of aiding in your recruitment efforts for your worship team.

Current Team Member Recruitment

You are only one person. There can never be more of you. Even with your ear to the ground, you will never know all there is to know about the people of your church. This truth is directly proportional to the size of your church. The bigger the church, the less you will know the details of your church family. While we should constantly strive to know our people and meet their needs as we are able, you have a given capacity and threshold of how much you can stay "in the know" on the people of your church.

If you truly want a great number of open pathways to your team and you desire to have the greatest pool of people to make their way to your team, then you have to begin to teach your current team members to actively be on the lookout for people that need encouragement to sign up for the worship team. This effort sometimes happens naturally by the few go-getters on your team but often times even your own team members will need reminding that the worship team is searching for new recruits.

You'll have to find times to intentionally teach your team to be looking for new folks. There is one occasion that is particularly useful which has already been mentioned. The Recruitment Day is a great time to remind your team members that they should be on the lookout for talented or interested folks and have them invite those people to the Recruitment Day. Not only will it help the success of the day, but the reminder helps to regularly remind your team about searching for other people in the church body that could serve. Otherwise, the reminder to the team might be something you need to calendar to include in whatever method you use to communicate important matters to your team. My team has some time carved out at every rehearsal to go over important matters like this and we call this time Rehearsal Notes, but emails and newsletters work well also.

I also make it a priority that if someone does bring me the name of someone who they know is a musician or is interested in tech I will reach out to that individual directly just a single time to make an invite to sign up to serve with our worship team. This can be as simple as an email or phone call, but I make the invitation. This way you are actively recruiting people in your church and not hoping or assuming they know they're welcome.

One important matter to consider as well is you will get more of what you celebrate within your organization. If someone on your team does successfully have someone sign up for the team, even if the recruit doesn't work out for some reason, I make sure to celebrate publicly the individual who did the recruiting. It demonstrates to the team the culture of team recruitment and it encourages everyone to step up their individual efforts. I'll leave it to you to figure out how to celebrate someone for this but find ways to make it a big deal and make the celebration something memorable for the entire team. If you want your team to be helping you keep people streaming through the door you have to demonstrate how much it means to you to have them involved in the process.

Leaving Holes

One more quick tip. Don't clear empty roles off your platform.

If you're missing a synth player or a guitar player for a week, consider leaving the gear in place without someone in place to play it. It's a visual trigger to members of your congregation that there is a gap in your team and space for people to plug in. Not always, but occasionally leave an empty hole on your platform. Periodically conveying the need visually will drive someone to signup to fill the noticeable gap. We all want clean and tidy platforms for worship but this technique is a very clear open door to your team for someone with talent.

While this isn't an exhaustive list of the ways in which you can share with your people that the door to the worship ministry is open, you've hopefully realized the importance of combatting the idea that your team is full. You must be intentional about combatting this perception in your church because otherwise your ministry will come to be known as simply a clique for a few select favorite people and trust me, that's not a reputation you want for your ministry. Anything that is perceived as exclusive in the church tends to be viewed by the body as unhealthy and a source of division. Make sure your team is marked by inclusivity as often as you can.

5 – Are Certain People Right or Wrong for a Worship Team

Therefore, accept each other just as Christ has accepted you so that God will be given glory.

Romans 15:7 NLT

One aspect of being a worship leader I had to wrestle with very early on in my years of leading worship teams in the church was figuring out whether people who fall into certain categories were appropriate to be on the worship team. Part of our job as worship leaders is to help protect the integrity and reputation of the church and thereby protect the platform and who is elevated on it. The reality is the moment someone steps foot on to the platform during a worship service, most people in the crowd assume that person must be spiritually mature and have things put together as a person. Now the reality is we are all broken people, and no one is perfect, but we should take care to be aware of who we have participating with us on the worship team and their impact on the witness of our church. While I'm not advocating a merit-based system, there is value in considering where people are on their spiritual journey. This makes you a better leader and better pastor because you can help walk alongside people wherever they find themselves on their journey with Christ. Some people are ready for the privilege of being viewed as a leader in the church and some aren't. It is important here to note that I'll be giving my thoughts and opinions on some of the categories of folks who sign up to serve on your teams but in all cases, you should differ to standards your church has in place and the discernment and preferences of your lead pastor.

New Believers

Success! Your church has brought a lost person home and saved a soul! This baby-Christian is on fire for the Lord and wants to conquer the world for Christ. They are sold-out on Jesus and looking for a way to share their newfound life and passion. They have a whole lot of excitement and a truckload of spiritual immaturity to go with it. They probably have little theological understanding and honestly still pretty much look like every other heathen out there. And good news, when they signed up to serve in the church in response to their being re-born, they signed up for just about everything (except nursery duty, I mean really, nobody volunteers for that "duty"). The new believer wants to be on the worship team and lead from the platform and now you're wrestling with whether they're ready or not. Can they be trusted with the leadership that results from being visible on your church's platform?

New believers should be welcomed into ministry. We are all called to serve in the church, and we should never discourage the obedience of any believer. Discernment, however, is key to assessing whether someone who has just come to Christ in faith is ready to be one of your leaders from the platform. We'll discuss the impact of your team's witness later in this book but suffice it to say that we must be careful who we are elevating to a visible role on the platform. With new believers, you're going to need to spend some time getting to know the individual and assessing their witness. Some new believers quickly grab onto repentance and the Holy Spirit does a great work in them to turn them from sinful behaviors and lifestyles while others struggle to leave the path they had been walking. This is a time where your leadership and influence can make a difference in someone's spiritual journey. You will need to be intentional in keeping up with a new believer's discipleship journey. You want to make sure you spend time getting to know their story and their spiritual condition. This is not something you can guess on. It takes time and it requires questioning and listening. You may need to insist that someone attend your church's new believer course or you yourself may need to spend some time discipling them one-on-one. You may have to tell someone that they can't be on the platform during worship until they're no longer living with someone outside of marriage. Whatever the case may be, there's no need to exclude anyone from joining the team merely because they've only just been saved.

New believers bring a few interesting dynamics to any ministry team. New believers bring a whole lot of enthusiasm and fire that can be infectious to other more mature believers that have lost a bit of zeal. New believers also force us to revisit our own beliefs as their questions arise. New believers can also be challenging as their excitement for Jesus can sometimes lead them to feel not enough is being done by the church to evangelize or do works of compassion or that the church isn't acting quickly enough. Their newfound faith can bring great energy but will also need a lot of guidance and encouragement from more mature believers.

When it comes to new believers, I suggest allowing them to join the team if they have the talent and the heartbeat to serve the church. What better way for someone to grow in spiritual maturity than to hang out with other mature believers? Insist that a new believer participate in some sort of new believer class or Bible Study. I also suggest you pair the new believer with a veteran of your team. Have them hang out together a lot for a while when your team meets. This should take place for a couple of months. If your worship team rotates volunteers like mine does, then you may want several people spending time with the new believer as a partner. This partnership should encourage the new believer as they won't feel alone in their new spiritual journey with Jesus but also ensures someone other than just you is keeping tabs on their growth. Also, I would avoid giving the new believer too much of a public role very early on. Allow them the time to learn the ropes of ministry and time to learn their witness matters with people in the church and outside the church. This time will also allow them to observe other believers and how they live the Christian walk week in and week out. Above all, help them learn to love Jesus more deeply. He will do most of the work moving them from spiritually immature to seasoned believer. Show them how much you love Jesus and how your life reflects it.

Non-Believers

This group of people is more challenging to decide if they belong serving on a worship team and is probably the most polarizing group. Can someone who is not saved and doesn't profess Jesus as savior be allowed to help lead a service in church? Seems like a conflict of interest, doesn't it? Well, if you haven't experienced it yet you likely will someday. If you're doing things with excellence in your ministry, your team will be attractive to all types who might want to be involved.

So how do you handle someone who doesn't believe in Jesus but wants to serve His church? Should you just respond with an automatic no? My advice is to begin with their motivation. Ask them point blank why they want to be on the team. Then you can assess what they're after. I legitimately had someone volunteer years ago who wasn't a believer but his whole family was believers, and they all went to church together and he wanted to be a good dad and be a part of what his family did. He was a great bass player and he saw a way for himself to contribute to what his family was excited about, their church. Not a terrible motivation for him to want to play in our worship band. The decision for me became easy to make, I allowed him to audition and serve. He made our band sound better and our worship service quality improved. But I didn't let his participation go unchecked. I required him to attend our church's membership class to ensure he knew our church values and didn't do anything to tarnish the church's mission or witness. I also had him abide by the Worship Arts Team Covenant that all our team members sign and uphold (we'll discuss this covenant in a future chapter). I was upfront with him about needing to act like a believer even if he wasn't one at heart in order to protect the integrity of our ministry. While I wish I could say he came to believe and was saved, his family moved before he ever made a decision to accept Jesus as Lord. But I witnessed strides in his life that certainly gave him greater awareness of Jesus and His gospel of grace and salvation, and it certainly improved his home life being asked to live by Christian principles and our church's values.

I've also experienced a young man who been an avid atheist most of his life join our team. He'd recently been through very difficult times and had realized his ways of doing things had led to most of the disaster that was his life. He came to us seeking a better way forward and we included him on our Production Team. I'm happy to say that after some time being exposed to our team's influence the guy accepted Christ as Lord and Savior and set his life upon a different course.

The lesson here is to be straightforward with non-believers. Ask tough questions and gain a clear understanding of why the individual wants to be a part of something they don't actually believe in. Also, set the accountability bar high. You want to protect your church, its leaders, and its ministries. But again, I tend to feel like if there's any way to bring non-believing people closer to a group of people who love Jesus, I'm going to find a way to make sure there is a place for them to get to know Jesus better. There's no better way for this to take place than on-going exposure like this.

Youth

Youth can be awfully tricky when it comes to worship ministry. For our purposes of discussion let's define youth as a young person who is in the school ages of sixth grade through twelfth grade. On the one hand, youth typically bring energy, excitement, and fresh eyes, ears, and ideas. On the other hand, youth bring inexperience, impatience, and at times unreliability. Do the benefits outweigh negatives? The answer is unfortunately a bit subjective. There are some matters where you as ministry leader will have to use your judgement and the judgements of others to decide if a youth should serve as a part of your worship team.

The first thing I'd share with you is that it is my opinion that you should have a culture of including youth in your ministry whenever possible. The statistical reality is that many youth leave the church when they graduate high school and a contributing factor is they don't feel included in the church as a whole. They may feel they belong to your church's youth group but as soon as they graduate from high school and can't be a part of the youth group, they will feel alienated from church if they haven't already been integrated into its total church ministries. If we are to disciple the next generation the way we should be, then we have to include teaching them to love serving in the church and not just be a part of a great youth program. Teaching them to be engaged in ministry translates to them being lifelong contributors to the body and not just consumers. Whatever ways you can find to encourage this should be pursued. If they are planted in your church you will find that your church's youth will remain planted in church, even ones that go off to college. You'll likely find one of the first things they do is seek out a church to plug into during their college years if they have been included in the ministries of the total church during their formative years. As well, when new visitors to your church witness youth participating in the ministries of worship gatherings it conveys that your church is vibrant and healthy and is concerned with ministering to the whole family.

After adopting a general sense of including youth in your worship teams, the first thing I consider when it comes to youth is a functional reality. The first question I have for a youth that wants to serve or for their parents is do they have consistent transportation. I have found through the years this to be the greatest hurdle for youth. This will also likely be your greatest frustration when it comes to youth. If they can't get a ride to rehearsal or Sunday services, then all of a sudden, you've got a gap in your team that you might have otherwise been able to fill. Youth are not known for planning ahead well and this issue tends to come up at the last minute. There are few things more frustrating than trying to chase down a ride for someone thirty minutes before a rehearsal or service. Let me also add a warning here. If you are a certain type of person then your spirit in this moment is probably urging you to simply think you'll just pick them up and give them a ride if they can't get there on their own.

Please don't make this mistake. I commend you for your generosity and your willingness to ensure someone can participate. However, it has been my experience that when someone becomes dependent on you for their ride it quickly turns into a source of frustration for you and your ministry. This is true of someone at any age honestly, but youth tend to face this issue more regularly because they might not drive themselves yet and their parents may be career focused leaving the youth to work things out on their own. I find that the time right before services and rehearsals more specifically are critical times for you as a leader to be prepping to engage in ministry and when you are giving that time away to going to get someone or wait on someone who is not ready to leave, matters of ministry will fall through the cracks. Your best use of that time is spent getting yourself prepared for all that you need to be doing. Being helpful occasionally is ok and you'll survive as a leader, but you simply cannot be someone's long-term solution.

The next thing I urge you to consider when evaluating a youth is their commitment level. It has been my experience that there is seldom a gray area when it comes to a youth's commitment level, they are either flaky or are very devoted. You obviously don't want the headache of flakes on your team, so it is best to weed out the flakes early. There are two aspects to gauging how committed a youth might be. The first is have they at all demonstrated any commitment in their life elsewhere? Many times, you can better discern whether a youth will be committed if they have actively shown they can be depended on. This might mean they have volunteered elsewhere in your church consistently. It might mean they can demonstrate involvement in a club or sport at school or even having held some type of job over a long enough time period. The rule here is if they can't follow through somewhere else, they likely won't follow through for you. This is an important conversation to have with a youth and their parents before you begin your process of getting them plugged into the ministry. It is important to convey the level of commitment you expect upfront so youth know it is important for them to follow through on their commitments and any consequences of not meeting team expectations. The other matter to consider falls at the opposite end of the spectrum. Youth tend to be *very* busy in our current culture. There are many activities and responsibilities competing for their attention. In reality, many youth I interact with are way over-scheduled. While many of the activities kids are involved with are great and probably look fantastic on college applications, it keeps them very busy and very scattered honestly. It is beneficial to you and your team to make sure a youth truly has the time required to be involved in your ministry which requires a time commitment on their part. I am personally burdened in my ministry to not contribute to the extreme level of busyness that our families face today so I look to make sure that youth in particular have the time required to practice, attended rehearsal, serve in services, and participate in some of the other aspects of our worship ministry and other ministry in the church at large. You don't want to be frustrated by spending your time and effort getting a youth ready to serve only to have them unavailable or ineffective because of their lack of focus. Trust me when I say you would much rather have fewer committed folks than an abundance of flakes on your team. You can do more with excellence than with sheer numbers.

You should also be careful to evaluate a young adult's maturity level before joining your team. This is *highly* subjective. My advice here is born from the reality that our worship team spends a small portion of our rehearsals every week in a brief Bible Study and Prayer Time (we'll get into an effective rehearsal schedule in a later chapter with more detail on this time together). We spend time diving into God's word together and praying for each other and for our church, its leaders, our services, and our community. Sometimes these conversations can get deep and at times our prayer time can be intense as we really dive into each other lives. In these times as we are real with one another we face really good topics that we praise God for but we also face deep challenges as we seek to walk with the Lord particularly as a group of adults. Maturity level matters a lot here as we wrestle with matters that require spiritual maturity and confidentiality. This environment has to be open and safe to truly work and some youth just may not be old enough or emotionally or spiritually developed enough to handle this time appropriately. It is an absolute must that you discuss this reality with both the youth and whoever cares for them and knows them best. As you hopefully know, some kids are wise beyond their years, they possess a wisdom and maturity that can only be a gift from the Holy Spirit. You'll know quickly that they will join the group with no issues. Other kids you may not know well or know they couldn't handle that environment and it is best to protect them from a compromising situation. My advice is if there is any doubt, make them wait and find another area for them to serve and contribute in the church.

Fortunately, there is somewhere to send them and not just issue a "no" and a closed door. If your church doesn't already have some version of a youth worship team, then I encourage you to get one going *yesterday*! In addition to being a blessing to your church in a number of ways, youth leading worship services for youth events, or even your main church service, has several benefits that directly benefit the health and growth of your primary worship team at your church. The church should be in the business of raising up the next generation of the church which means it should also be serious about the business of raising up the next generation of worshippers and worship leaders. Having a youth worship team is absolutely vital in this aim. Again, style matters little here so whether it be a worship band or vocal choir or whatever your church's model, having a place for youth to participate in leading worship must be a part of your church's ongoing ministries.

There are two benefits of having this ministry that directly impact your worship team. As mentioned before, having somewhere to direct students who may not be old enough or mature enough will do wonders for the credibility of your leadership. When you have somewhere to get kids plugged in it says you're serious about involving youth in ministry. You are able to make sure no one falls through the cracks in your church. This environment allows for those not mature enough for your main worship team to have a space and time to be disciples and grow and mature. You can't be accused of not investing in the next generation and you can't be accused of being exclusive. Trust me, it happens with those who you might have to say no to. The other benefit is that over a long enough time arc, a youth team serves as a farm club for future adult worship leaders. When you get kids hungry for serving in the worship ministry, they will naturally want to migrate over to the more adult oriented worship ministries. If you want a regular influx of new servants for your team that come with experience and a comfort level for leading worship services, then you want a youth worship team where kids can develop these skills in an environment suited to their age bracket. You can also spend these years instilling the culture of your team so they will fit in from day one on your main worship team. If your church runs multiple worship environments through the week, the youth team also serves as another pool from which to schedule volunteers to make sure all your services are staffed. I can't encourage you enough to make the investment in spending time with students building them into your worship leaders of tomorrow. You should not overlook this important aspect of your oversight of worship ministries. This also serves as a great opportunity for your adult volunteers to mentor young people as well. You likely also find your youth trying some new things with music or technology that you'll want to take note of, learn from, and incorporate into your own bag of tricks. They really will help keep your ministry young, vibrant, and relevant, something all artists have to be intentional about.

Church-Hoppers

Of the categories of who's right for a worship team, this category is the easiest one for me personally to consider. If you haven't met someone in this category yet I have no doubt that you will eventually. In this modern era, particularly in America, we live in a culture where everyone is accustomed to being able to have access to the things that they want and exactly how they want them. We also have a church on almost every street corner which means people's options are plentiful when choosing a church to attend. This means there are people who bounce from church to church looking for the Goldilocks church or even people who cherry pick which aspects of which churches to attend…simultaneously. For me I try to head off church-hoppers whenever I can and protect my ministry team from this category.

There are a couple of problems that present themselves with this type of potential worship team member. I am convinced that in light of the apostle Paul's teachings in the New

Testament on being a member of the body of Christ as a part of His church, that we are called to belong to a body of believers. The implication for belonging is being *present*. How can one belong to something if they are not, quite simply, present to be a part of whatever is going on? Being a member of the body means contributing to the greater whole. This means being active in all areas of ministry and mission within the local church. You can't remove a hand and have it function or have it be any benefit to the function of the rest of the body. And once severed it is only through the marvels of modern medicine that a hand *might* be able to be reattached. I stand firmly upon the conviction that anyone in the church should be fully committed to their church where they feel called. Do we move among bodies of believers as we go through life? Of course we do, it's the nature of life for a whole host of reasons. But once planted in a church God calls people to be fully committed to that church so that they can be fully engaged in knowing and being known, loving and being loved, ministering to and being ministered to. When you combine this with the reality that most church congregations see their worship team members as leaders in the church due to their position on the public platform, having worship team members not fully engaged becomes problematic and can lead to feelings of confusion, resentment, and division. These are feelings you want to do everything to avoid so that you protect your church and the hearts of its members. The visible nature of being on a worship team necessitates that worship team members do not have a divided church life.

I also believe in a high level of accountability with my worship team members. We work hard, we play hard, and it all works to glorify God in our local setting and the team thrives but only because we have high standards for commitment and preparation. This is really hard to enforce with people who are attending multiple churches at the same time. My advice is ask anyone who you suspect of being a church hopper about their intentions to fully dive into being committed to your church. If they waver at all or resist being fully invested in your church, politely inform them that until they can make a full commitment to your church, you will prefer to hold off on including them in the worship ministry at your church. This can be a challenging conversation if you never had to handle one of these, but the hard conversation will more often times than not move the church-hopper to a fully committed church member which benefits all parties concerned.

Now, what about someone who has just started coming to your church and hasn't been there very long at all? Do you consider them a church-hopper? The simple truth is you just have to get to know them and find out if they are in the process of fully plugging into your church or if they are just testing the waters and want to be involved with the worship ministry to look under the hood. Use your best judgement and get input from other church staff and lay leadership as to whether or not they are plugging in around the church. Being new shouldn't be a disqualifying factor but figure out why they are new. Were they disgruntled at their last church? Why? Were they *looking* for something to be unhappy about? Those people do exist. People who look for things to be wrong will find something wrong at your church, too, no matter how much you love your church and can embrace its strengths and weaknesses. Or did they have a legitimate reason for feeling called to look for a new church home? Church-hopping can demonstrate a lack of spiritual maturity that you want to protect your team from, but you may also have met someone that is generally excited about their new church family and what God has in store for them. It's your job to find out their story but again be weary of those just bouncing from church to church to suit their *own* needs. They tend to not be strongly committed anywhere they go and can fall off the planet in a single moment and you'll never hear from them again, which is really frustrating.

Paid Musicians and Production Team

In my experience this category tends to come up most often in new church launches or in small churches that are trying to aggressively grow. The topic of whether or not to pay people to be in critical positions in a worship band, critical musicians like an organist, or on the Production Team tends to arise most in small church environments where there are fewer people to field a full team. The challenge to the concept of offering compensation for talent usually arises from a well-meaning church attendee, maybe even someone involved in the worship ministry, who feels paying someone to serve in church appears unbiblical and feels inappropriate. I have personally heard several people through the years object and offer the solution that certain roles should be filled with volunteers. But what happens when you simply don't have that volunteer and no prospects on the horizon? Is going without meeting the need the spiritual answer? It is true God provides for our needs and sometimes we need to wait on His timing. But I also believe God meets needs in ways that we don't anticipate and don't think of when we first consider a challenge we are facing. I don't personally believe God wants us to sacrifice giving Him our best efforts and offerings just because we are waiting. How long can your church's worship experiences limp along with critical roles vacant? If you are committed to excellence in your church's worship services and its programming, the answer is not very long. People will notice elements of your services underperforming and may feel led to look elsewhere for services that are more organized or better executed. Remember, excellence is attractive, mediocrity is off-putting.

While it should be ideal to have your worship teams fully staffed by volunteer members of your congregation and a worthwhile goal to constantly pursue, it is a disservice to our churches to be satisfied with incomplete rosters. The vision for our services can only be carried out by people in place, serving and ministering to our congregations and there may come a time when you may need to consider paying someone to fill in a gap that your church just doesn't have someone local to fill yet. This might mean something short-term like just filling a spot for a week, or it may mean something long-term that you may need to adequately plan for in your worship ministry budget year to year.

I once served with a unique ministry based out of Jacksonville, FL that dealt with this very reality. The ministry is called Ascension Worship Network. The ministry builds a network of artists and people skilled with production and A/V who love serving in worship. Churches can contact Ascension and request people to fill the gaps they might have for their worship services. I served primarily as someone who could actually show up and lead a service as a "front guy", or primary worship leader, but you can request anything from drummers to sound engineers. It's a great resource and the network has spread to many of the larger cities around the country. There's a reasonable fee for having someone from Ascension come to fill in at your church but it was a blessing as an artist to serve in the ministry when I did, and it has been a blessing to my ministry in the local church to have such an awesome resource to fill gaps when the need arises.

Ultimately, any paid person really should be a short-term solution. If you're serious about building your worship team you'll want the team made up of folks who know your church, its mission and values, and its people. This really is best and the most effective way for your Worship Team to be active ministers of the gospel in your church. People who are bought in to your vision and not just there for a paycheck will always carry out your church's mission more effectively. My advice is to fill the gaps as you need with someone who is paid to ensure you have a quality worship experience but always be moving towards replacing paid folks with volunteer church family members. This does not, however, apply to staff roles that your ministry needs as it grows larger. As your church, and hopefully your ministry, grows there will come times when you and your church leadership will identify key positions that are better suited for part-time or full-time paid staff. There are just some jobs that require more hours and more attention. These church jobs obviously should be compensated competitively. I am referring to the skill positions within the team that ultimately can't be filled with your own church members. These might be additional worship leaders, music directors, or production directors.

You will no doubt encounter these categories of prospects for your Worship Team. Hopefully this gives you direction on who to target for recruiting and also some guidance on some of the trickier types of folks who may find their way into your Worship Team sign-ups. Obviously, you will encounter unique folks who didn't fit any category or mold. Get to know the people God sends you and allow the Holy Spirit to guide you with discernment as you work towards getting people engaged in your Worship Team. Not everyone will always work out, but the good news is that's ok. Some people are just not a great fit for serving on a worship team even if they are talented. Your job is to foster a great ministry team, not a great house band so it's ok to screen some people out along the way. Your team should be known for being inclusive, but you can be inclusive and also have high standards and you don't have to apologize for that or fit in every person in that comes along.

6 – An Audition Process

Give all your worries and cares to God, for he cares about you.

1 Peter 5:7

No one enjoys being analyzed, evaluated, and critiqued. There is nothing fun about sticking yourself out there for someone else to make a subjective judgment call about your abilities or qualities. For most people, auditions cause crushing amounts of anxiety and worry. Don't believe me? Show up to a random audition and look for the physical shaking found in most people there. You'll find it, I promise. The shaking is because of the very real fear these people are experiencing.

And yet holding auditions is an essential part of ensuring the quality level of groups or teams that require some expression of the arts. For a talent-based group, holding an audition allows those in charge to see if someone can perform the needed skills to participate. And if you're overseeing the music at your church you need to be auditioning people for your teams, especially key vocalists and instrumentalists. If you're running a traditional choir your need for auditions may be different but I'd still recommend an audition process for the long-term benefit of your ministry and programs. The only way to elevate program quality is to insist upon elevating the talent level.

People, however, *hate* auditions. Even among professional artists and actors, only a few truly enjoy the experience of being on display for the purpose of making the cut for some project. Most of us hate the idea. We're terrified of being told we don't have the chops to be a part of something we're interested in, and rightly so. It's a basic human need to be accepted and the potential rejection inherent in an audition makes us all nervous and anxious, and for some of us…nauseous.

Throughout my life I've been involved in numerous aspects of performing arts. Almost all of them exposed me to submitting to auditions. I've done choirs in church, in schools, and in the community. I've done theater, barbershop quartets, handbell choirs, and I've even auditioned for a national talent agency. I've experienced very casual environments and I've experienced highly competitive and professional situations. I've also conducted numerous auditions along the way as well. They're seldom fun and seldom does anyone feel good about what they've accomplished during an audition. The truth is that being nervous and uptight always impacts performance and people rarely ever do the very best they have to offer in an audition. That fear of rejection is nagging and persistent and gets the best of the best of us. Combined with the reality that most folks you'll encounter wanting to join your worship team are merely church volunteers and not professional artists with loads of audition experience, telling your church people you want them to submit to audition can potentially scare people off or at best make them extremely uneasy.

So how do we as worship ministry leaders strike a balance? I can't stress enough the importance of having a process for evaluating the skills of worship team prospects as a means to improving the quality of your team but we also have to be sensitive to the fact that we are working with volunteers who may be uneasy about putting themselves out there for critique. The answer rests in moving away from what I call the "one-and-done" audition to an audition process. The one-and-done is the typical model for an audition which involves having people show up to a single time slot, they demonstrate their talent somehow in front somebody or a group staring at them, and then someone or a group makes a decision either on the spot or at a later time. No one does their A+ best under these circumstances. It's incredibly intimidating and awkward. We're stripped bare, and our talent or lack thereof is totally exposed and vulnerable. An *audition process* makes it possible for people to truly demonstrate what they have to offer and what they are capable of with a bit less pressure and vulnerability. Making your volunteers more comfortable is a huge win with the audition process but the process my team and I have developed over the years has resulted in multiple other benefits for our worship team as well. The rest of this chapter will outline the benefits and will explain the system we use for our audition process. Our process is not perfect, and it certainly is not the only means to conduct auditions but it has worked exceedingly well for years and if you are in need of a system to conduct auditions or want to make your existing system better then please use whatever you can to help improve this aspect of the worship ministry at your church. Remember to customize as needed for your unique situation. Our square peg may not fit into your round hole.

The Benefits

Through the years our goal was to make auditions more approachable for the average church volunteer musician interested in joining the worship team. I've lost track of the number of times I have seen the look of panic or angst on the face of a worship team prospect melt away when they hear about our audition process and that it is not a one-and-done audition. The idea of only having one shot is terrifying but the idea of having time to prepare, observe, and then perform is comforting to most of the average volunteers who will come your way. The unknown is scary to people, but our process gives people the opportunity to unravel the mystery before stepping out to be evaluated. This is really a matter of ministry because we should have compassion for the anxiety of auditions and care enough for our people to not put them through that if we can help it. As well, the unintended consequences of the audition process have proved invaluable for the growth and health of the worship ministries I have overseen. The results have been team members who are more prepared, committed, and invested in the success of our ministry mission and greater transparency and credibility for my own leadership.

One of the best aspects of our system is it allows us to set the bar high early. Our process requires that people demonstrate they can meet the basic requirements of being on the team. We do not ask our recruits to do anything we do not ask our team members to do, and this allows us to see whether people can handle serving on our worship team. But we do expect that they can prepare and perform in exactly the same way they would as if they were on the team. If they can't keep up during the audition process, then we know for sure they will not be able to keep up on an ongoing basis as a member of the team. When you are doing the one-and-done approach, you cannot evaluate things like commitment, punctuality, preparedness, and consistency over a time arc. You can't get this kind of information about people with a one-and-done.

The audition process also allows us to get to know people better. As a ministry leader or pastor, knowing your people in a more intimate way allows you to be a better shepherd. Part of our process allows time for not only you as leader but your team members as well to get to know folks more deeply before making a decision. Knowing where people are coming from and where they are on their spiritual journey allows you to better understand and care for the people God brings to your ministry. Remember, your job is not to be the best musician but rather the best servant. Artists can be unique and even weird folks and knowing people's unique quirks and hang-ups can help protect you, your team, and the person auditioning from difficult or unforeseen situations. You'll also quickly discover if unique and weird people will fit into how your team operates. We all love free spirits, but rebellious spirits can be destructive to the effectiveness and momentum of your ministry team. Be ok with weird, don't be ok with rebellious. These people will stick out early rather than later and you can manage the situation before someone gets too deeply involved in the team and causes too much harm to team or church unity. It also makes you a better leader when you can know people more intimately and know their strengths and weaknesses which ultimately allows you to position your team members for success and not ask them to do more than they are currently capable of. You'll also know better where to challenge your people for growth both in their artistic craft but also in spiritual growth. It's probably best not to have a baby Christian leading up front just yet or someone who's only been playing guitar for nine months to play that Lincoln Brewster screaming guitar solo. You and your team will only know that if you spend the time getting to know people well.

Our audition process also aids in building involvement and investment from your current team members. I am a huge believer and proponent of team ministry. If you want your team to grow and to be healthy and not based solely on you, you must include people in the systems of your ministry. Your job is to build disciples and that means having others involved in the business of how your team operates. Our process includes our entire team in the evaluation and the decision-making process.

This means your team has skin in the game with regards to who joins the team. Their concern in the matter means they take seriously the privilege they have as leaders on the platform in your church and they take seriously the responsibility of protecting the integrity and quality of what is presented during services from your church's platform. It also means you do not have to be the only set of eyes and ears evaluating people. You are only one person and you can't be in multiple places at once or listening to or watching multiple people simultaneously. If the recruiting efforts we discussed earlier go as planned, its not unheard of to have multiple people to evaluate during your rehearsal at one time simultaneously (I'll explain how people auditioning fit into rehearsals in a moment). It may take time to build trust in your people to carry out this role and to teach them the things to look and listen for but once the culture grabs hold, you'll be amazed how capable your people can be at helping make these kinds of decisions. I've stood around with my team and heard them talk about terminology like diction, stage presence, musicality, and worship attitude without my prompting. Remember, these are my *volunteers*! It's a beautiful thing to watch when it starts clicking.

Another benefit I'm particularly fond of is that our process provides a layer of protection for you as ministry leader. A long time ago, before I had the process we use in place there were several times I was accused of playing favorites, excluding people, or stacking the worship team with only the best talent and holding back mid-level talent. When I was making the decisions by myself, I opened myself up to these types of attacks. The accusations broke my heart because my passion lies at the complete opposite end of these ungodly motivations. By having a process for auditions and by including the team at large in the final decision process, it's exceedingly difficult for someone to accuse you as the pinnacle of your ministry of those kinds of behaviors that admittedly don't belong in the church. Your credibility is protected because you have a team to back you up. In fact, if you adopt the process, the final decision rests entirely out of your hands and in the hands of the rest of the worship team. You, of course, have oversight, but the final call is not on your shoulders. This has been so comforting and encouraging to me through my years of conducting auditions to know I have this layer of protection against naysayers and disgruntled prospects who didn't make the cut. It also provides a clear system to point to how decisions are made which provides a healthy measure of transparency to your personal leadership and minimizes the subjective nature of auditions.

If you've been in ministry for any period of time, this all hopefully sounds pretty appealing. Happier prospects, engaged and invested team members, protection for your leadership; it's not too good to be true, I promise. At the time of writing this book I've been using this audition process for fifteen years and the proof is in the results. I've used this system in multiple ministry settings, and it works time after time. Hopefully you're sold at this point so let's walk through what the audition process system looks like.

An Audition Process

Over-Communicate Upfront

The first thing I do with worship team sign ups is tell them what to expect. I tend to be an over-communicator and its due to my experience. I have found through the years that the more people know what to expect the more at ease they are with experiencing something new. You don't necessarily need to give *all* the nuts and bolts of your team's audition process, but you definitely want to provide the road map for how someone joins the worship team. I've learned that over-communication eases fears and begins to unravel the mystery and the unknown. People fear the unknown, but you can proactively remove their fears by giving details. This can be done if you meet a prospect at church or through a phone call or even an email. I tend to do some combination of these. I tell people face to face when I first have the chance to meet them, and I also have an email template setup that I send whenever I send a schedule request email for someone to come to their audition. Sometimes it takes people hearing the process a time or two to feel less anxious about what they are stepping into. Another important thing I do is to make sure I give people a way to contact me directly and I tell them that it is my job to help them through the process. I tell them to contact me whenever they need help for any reason even if it is just to ask simple questions. When people know someone will be there to hold their hand they tend to be more at ease. Not everyone will need to bug you, in fact most won't, but for a few people knowing they can get a hold of you calms a lot of fears about submitting to the audition process.

The Test Drive

The Test Drive isn't something you have to offer everyone that comes your way but it can be a useful tool to keep in your back pocket to capture someone who may be nervous about jumping in or committing or for someone who is curious about whether they would be a fit on the worship team. The Test Drive can look like a couple things. It may be inviting a prospect to come and observe rehearsal. This can give people a taste of how your team operates and what would be expected of them. I find that little bit of connection to the team and witnessing how much fun we have serving together is enough to get people hooked and want to get involved. Letting them peel back the curtain and view that we are genuine in how we prepare and how we lead during services buys us credibility as well. The Test Drive may be as simple as letting someone get connected to the resources you use. Through the years we've had a few musicians come our way that want to see what kind of studio charts we use and whether they would be comfortable using them for playing. Our church uses Planning Center to plan and organize our services and resources. I can't recommend Planning Center enough, if you're not using worship planning software of some kind you should be (we'll discuss this more in a future chapter). It's no skin off my back to allow someone access to our Planning Center portal for a week or so for them to poke around and see what resources we have to offer.

Letting people "look under the hood" or "kick the tires" allows them to build a comfort level with you and your ministry. Remember, you're trying to remove the fear that comes with auditions so anything you can do to make prospects more comfortable you should make some effort to do. During this Test Drive time you can also begin evaluating whether these folks communicate well i.e. checking email or texts. You can also gauge will they follow through with commitments like showing up to a rehearsal time, do they show up early or late, and do they come with a good attitude. This opportunity can help you get some extra time to get to know the personalities and habits of your potential team members. Don't feel like you need to obnoxiously chase people who are flaky, but you can certainly allow people to only put one foot through the door before coming in. Keep in mind people want to know their precious time is invested well if they are going to commit to something so letting them observe and poke around a bit will help them realize your ministry is worth investing in.

The One-on-One Portion

We start all musicians out with a one-on-one portion of our Audition Process. This part somewhat looks like a typical audition because it's useful for evaluating people's individual talent level. However, by calling it a one on one, it seems less intimidating to the average volunteer. It's not *the* audition, it's just the first part of the process. Be certain that you can still say "no" during this part of the process, but the prospect doesn't need to necessarily know that yet. You let the prospect know you'd like to hear them perform just by themself to make sure they can meet the basic requirements of the worship team. We plug our people into Planning Center and schedule them for a time to come in to demonstrate their musical skill. We typically send them two current worship songs via Planning Center for them to be prepared to sing, play, or both depending on their skill set. These songs are ones that we have backing tracks for. This really is the only time I use a full-on track in my ministry because it allows me to focus on the one person and their abilities, otherwise I prefer live music always. We use an internet-based service that provides tracks where I can mute individual instruments in the track for the purpose of the audition. For example, we can mute the bass track if we are auditioning a bass guitarist. By using the track I'm not worried about having to play with the prospect or keep a band together. I can just focus on the person and their music. There are no vocals so for singers it's basically karaoke.

When the prospect arrives, I get them set up on the mic or channel in our sound system and we do the music portion of the one on one right away. Almost everyone is nervous about performing and I find letting them get it out of the way quickly is best. They're ready to get it over with. They will play and/or sing along with the track with just myself present unless it is a member of the opposite sex and then I'll have either my wife or one of our female worship team members present just to hang out so that I'm not alone with a member of the opposite gender (a good policy to have for anyone in ministry to remain above reproach). I tend to sing with them here and there just to keep them on pace with the track and to give cues for song progression. I also try to show that I'm having fun listening to them and making music with them; it settles them a little to see me bobbing my head and worshipping. I have a form I use that has a 1- 5 scale for evaluating numerous aspects of music and performance such as tone, diction, musicality, preparedness, breathing, worship attitude, song awareness, stage presence, and more. Depending on what the person is auditioning for I may or may not use every category. My rule of thumb is if the majority of the categories are 3 and up then I'll pass the person along to the next part of our audition process. If the average is below 3 then I'll say it's a no go. We'll talk more about saying no later in this chapter. My mentality in this time is that I am looking for two things in people who show up for the one on one: 1. Do they show up prepared having done their homework? 2. Can they keep up with a band? If you're a talented musician and have some experience, you'll know the answers to these two questions quickly. I am not looking for superstars or perfection in this moment, I am looking for potential. Remember, this is going to feel really uncomfortable for just about everybody, they are not going to do their best in this environment. You want to gauge whether or not you think they would be able to handle the next portion of the process, which in our system is rehearsing with us; more on that in a moment.

Once the prospect has made it through the two songs, I might ask them if they have anything else they want to share. This especially applies to musicians and, in particular, drummers and bass guitarists who might have a great beat they could play or an awesome lick that might demonstrate a little more skill. A majority of worship songs aren't complex, let's be real. This is totally up to you but its nice sometimes to see more of what people have to offer. Once they're done with the music, I will have the prospect sit down with me so we can have a conversation.

The conversation time is where you can start to do ministry. This time is as much about business as it is about beginning to build relationships with people. This is some of the best time you will have with people, uninterrupted, to get to know them personally, their history, and what makes them tick. For me personally, our team is large and lots of things and people demand my attention at rehearsals and service times so I really treasure this time where I can get to know folks one on one. Here's a list of what I cover in this conversation:

1. Biographical Questions
    a. Favorite album/artist
    b. Favorite past time
    c. Spiritual heritage/history
2. Yes move on, or No not yet
    a. Things they did well
    b. Things to improve on
If Yes,
3. How the rest of the Audition Process works

4. Ask them to attend church's info/new member class
5. Talk about responsibilities and rewards of being a part of the worship team
    a. You'll be seen as a leader on and off the platform, be aware
    b. Other fun things the team does together as a family
6. If they're moving on in the Audition Process, ask about their coming schedule and availability to attend rehearsals

When I start this conversation, I like to immediately begin with the following question: "You are going to be stranded on a deserted island and you can only take one album, what would it be?" It usually catches them off guard because they think you're going to immediately talk about how *bad* they did with their music. It communicates that you want to get to know the person a little bit and that you like to have a little fun. I also like the question because it squeezes the person a little and forces them to really tell you what kind of music they're into and what they typically listen to. This can be really insightful as to their own music style and preferences and whether that would at all translate to worship music. I will ask a few other questions and then ask about their spiritual journey and heritage. This is your best opportunity to gauge a person's spiritual condition. Everything else in the conversation you can phrase to suit your own personality and systems but the most important thing to cover is your decision as to whether or not the person will move on to the rest of the Audition Process. For me this can potentially be the hardest part of my job…telling someone **no**. As someone who is really passionate about getting people involved in ministry there is almost no joy in telling someone "No" and they're not quite good enough. The only joy comes in knowing I am protecting my team's pursuit of excellence in worship by saying no. So, let's talk about saying no.

There's no great way to go about saying no in the church. But trust me that you want to get more comfortable doing so. If you want your team to get better and your ministry's quality to improve you need elevated standards and that means having to tell some folks they don't yet measure up. Notice I used the word *yet*. This lies at the heart of how I go about saying no to someone. I share with them what I thought they did well (yes sometimes you'll have to stretch for this, but you can find something to compliment) but then tell them where their skill set is lacking or where I've picked up on a spiritual maturity issue. It is important to not make musical critiques personal but rather about their skills or place on their spiritual journey. I also tend to spend more time talking about what they did well rather than what they need to work on. This is my way of caring for their heart. They may have a natural talent for music, it just may not be developed yet to the point where they can play with others in a band or sing for something organized like a worship service. I try to give very clear feedback of what they need to work on and at times will even suggest they take lessons or record themselves to hear themselves. The point is to give them something to work on and I tell folks they are welcome to come back after a few months and try again. We never close the door on people. We believe people can grow spiritually and develop their craft, so we never say an outright no. Most people leave a little disappointed, obviously, but I don't think anyone has ever left feeling crushed because I gave it my all to lift them up and give them something to reach for. These conversations are not easy to navigate at times, but it does work. This approach is how it works throughout our entire Audition Process. We never completely close the door on people, and we try to treat everyone with compassion and love. We also tell everyone thank you for auditioning and for putting themselves out there to be critiqued. We let them know that we know that that's a hard thing to do and appreciate their courage to do it. This approach is more about the person and less about the success of your own project. Believe it or not we've even had people tell us thank you for telling them no and for providing feedback for where they could improve. Sounds crazy doesn't it, someone thanking you for telling them no? This has convinced me the approach tends to work well and it does because we care enough about the person to handle their hearts carefully. Now here's the interesting fact good or bad; I've never had someone come back to re-audition. Not that it couldn't happen, but the process has shown that those that need to be weeded out because they just couldn't keep up with a worship team are threshed out.

By having your prospects go through this portion of the Audition Process you've learned a lot about them. You've learned if they'll actually check and respond to their email. This is huge for our team, if you can't email, you can't serve. There's too much communicated via email and Planning Center which relies on emails to have someone not respond to messages. You've learned if they can show up on time and show up prepared. You've learned some about their musical skill and you've learned about their personality traits and hopefully a good bit about where they are at on their spiritual journey with Jesus.

So, let's say you've done the One-on-One and you've got someone on your hands with great talent. Yay for you! Are they in now? Nope! Now is when you get the rest of your team involved. At this point they should move on to the Group Portion of the Audition Process.

The Group Portion

The Group Audition is just a fancy way of saying having the prospect participate at rehearsal. This is the point at which the rest of your team really takes over the audition process. Your prospect should be invited to attend rehearsal. The point here is to have the person auditioning do everything the rest of the team does on an ongoing basis. They're not on the team yet so they aren't required to serve at services, just attend rehearsal. But not just *a* rehearsal, two rehearsals.

So why two rehearsals? Well, for a couple reasons. The first reason is we feel that by giving someone two weeks to join us at rehearsal gives them more of a fair shot to do their best. A person may show up the first week and not know all the music, the people, our gear, our process, and our expectations. That's an extremely difficult environment for anyone to do their best and really demonstrate what they're capable of. By having a second week, people will come back the second week and have a better idea of what to expect and can show up and knock it out of the park. We also feel that by giving someone two weeks we can gauge how consistently can someone show up when they're supposed to, show up prepared consistently over multiple weeks, and if you rotate volunteers like our team does it gives more people the chance get to hear prospects play or sing and get the chance to know the person personally and spiritually. Someone could spend twelve hours the first week preparing and do great, but then life happens the second week and they only get thirty minutes to do homework for rehearsal and can't hack it. Two weeks equals more chances to succeed or fail and for more team members to recognize either of these results. The more people involved in the evaluation process to provide feedback the better. That way the decision is based on more than just one person's opinion. During this time, you should have the person auditioning do everything the rest of your team does including times of Bible study or prayer so you can see how they contribute to the team. If you have a full worship team, during rehearsal you may have to do some swapping in and out of certain positions. For instrumentalists, my advice is to rehearse until a song is ready for service and then swap in the person auditioning and give it a go with them. For vocalists, we utilize a worship choir, so a singer's time is spent in the worship choir until the second week. If the singer is interested in potentially being a lead featured vocalist, we'll swap them in on one of our songs during the second week that's appropriate for them to sing. We have a development process for lead vocalists so we aren't too concerned about whether they can make this cut yet but it is helpful for everyone to be able to specifically hear someone sing something for evaluation. After the first week's rehearsal with us we dismiss people auditioning for the night and tell them they are done and can leave, and we make sure to remind them that we as a team will be discussing their efforts once they leave. Make sure to make this reminder so that prospects know the whole team is making the decision, not just you. Remember, this is to help provide a layer of protection for your leadership. The second week we dismiss the prospect from the rehearsal space but have them hang out somewhere until we're done so that we can have a follow-up conversation with them before they leave for the night. For us, we send them to our Green Room which is right off of our worship stage. Wherever you send them, make sure it's somewhere they know how to get to. Once they're excused, we begin the After Discussion.

The After Discussion and the Vote

This time together as a worship team family really is pretty simple. We gather the whole team, and I mean everyone, present at rehearsal to discuss the people we're evaluating for the night. You'll want to make sure you leave some time at the end within your rehearsal schedule time to have these conversations. Don't wait until after rehearsal, your team will want to peace out and resent you making them stay for more stuff if you stay after rehearsal time. All members of our Platform Team and our Production Team hang around and share everything they heard, saw, and learned about the person auditioning with the purpose of making sure prospects are capable of being on the platform. This time is for you to facilitate discussion and not control the environment. This is the time for you to allow your worship team to have input and impact on the ministry. Ask follow-up questions and provide some input as needed but let your team do the evaluation. Having all team members part of this discussion is really vital. You'll be amazed, for example, at what your Production Team will hear from the sound system or see from a distance, even those who aren't musicians per se. They can notice important aspects of worship leading someone auditioning may or may not have as a part of their skill set.

When the conversation seems to wrap up then it's time to vote. Our system is a simple majority vote and we do it by simple thumbs up or thumbs down. I don't vote during this time, I'm just counting votes. For a person to pass the Group Portion of the Audition Process it requires a majority yes vote from both weeks. If you have a split vote between weeks, then you as ministry leader can exercise executive privilege and make the yes or no call. I've never had to make this call. We also have a policy that if someone is super talented and their heart is in the right place for worship and serving and we need them immediately we can vote to forgo the second week of audition and vote them straight onto the team. This requires a completely unanimous vote from the first week's team. This situation has happened only a couple of times in the years I've been using this Audition Process. I let this situation be instigated by people on the team and never by me but allow the process to play out if someone brings it up. It is a handy option to have though if someone comes along that could fill an immediate need. Again, building great teams means allowing their voice and feelings to have an impact on the direction of the ministry. Once you've gotten the results of the second week's vote then you need to go have the Follow Up Conversation with those who have completed the Group Portion of the Audition Process.

The Follow Up Conversation

Since we've already talked about saying no to someone, we'll assume for this section you're going to tell someone yes. These are some of the most exciting times of worship ministry for me. Being able to tell someone good job and the team voted them into the Platform Team of the worship ministry is great because you get to see someone be excited and relieved and encouraged all at once. Plus, it's a great feeling knowing you've got new blood on the team and that your team has grown! I'll take a moment to say congrats and thanks for submitting to the process and ask the new team member if they have any questions about their experience thus far.

The next task to complete is to let the new team member know what will happen next to get them ready to serve in worship services. This all starts by giving them our Worship Arts Team Orientation Packet. In my ministry, this is something we have all new worship team members go through. It is a packet that takes new members through some basic worship theology, team expectations, tips, dress codes, a few other matters of team culture, and finishes with our Worship Arts Team Covenant. Everyone who serves on our worship team must sign this covenant before being eligible to serve during our worship services. This includes our Production Team members before they complete their training period (I'll discuss both the packet and Production Team training strategies in future chapters). Once the Covenant is signed and returned then team members are eligible for to be scheduled to serve. We hand people the packet and let them know to go through the packet, pray about committing to our team expectations, and then sign and return the Covenant when they're ready. If the person is a vocalist, I also let them know the basics of our Vocalist Development Process which entails three months serving in our Worship Choir before having the potential to bump to a Lead Vocalist if they are interested in this role (I'll discuss this process more in a future chapter). I let vocalists know about this development process at this point to make sure a singer doesn't expect to take the spotlight their first week. This helps to make sure people are there for the right reasons. If they aren't interested in serving behind other Lead Vocalists from the Worship Choir first for a few months while they learn how our team operates, then they probably aren't going to fit into our "It's not about me" culture.

We also tell the new folks that there is no rush to serve. I am a firm believer in letting people decide when they're ready to serve on the platform. I never rush people. Just because they have made it through the Audition Process doesn't mean they're comfortable yet. People may appreciate some time to just rehearse with us for a time and knock the rust off or learn more music before jumping in. I tell people if they need a week or nine months, we're fine with it. Most people want to get going pretty quick. The important thing is to let people know that the ball is in their court. I want people to be blessed by serving and leading worship and forcing them to start before they're ready and comfortable runs the risk of them feeling overwhelmed, underprepared, and feeling embarrassed if they feel like they didn't do well in front of the whole church. Ask your new team members to let you or whoever manages scheduling for your ministry know when they are ready to start serving. If time allows, I'll pray with the person(s) and let them again know they can contact me anytime they need and that I am there to serve them and help equip them to serve in ministry and then say goodbye. The Audition Process is finished at this point, and you know you've got a great new team member on your hands that you have confidence will meet the requirements of your worship team.

Hopefully by now you've asked the question "What about Worship Team prospects who aren't musicians? What do I do with someone who signs up and wants to help with A/V and how do I get them connected?" In the next chapter, I'll talk about Production Teams and how we connect and engage those that want to help in worship but aren't musicians and don't need to Audition.

7 – The Production of a Production Team

Work willingly at whatever you do, as though you were working for the Lord rather than for people. Remember that the Lord will give you an inheritance as your reward, and that the Master you are serving is Christ.

Colossians 3:23-24

One person. The last *two* churches I was called to serve at…one person. That's how many people were serving on the Production Team at each church when I arrived. One church was a church of 100, the other 700. Both had only one person to run lights, sound, the presentation of lyrics and sermon slides, and run web casting. If you're struggling to get volunteers for this ministry, you're not alone. I've been there, I got the T-shirt, I'd like to return the shirt because it's not a fun place to be.

If there is any universal truth about contemporary worship services in the developed world it is that it relies heavily on the usage of multimedia. Lighting, sound design, computer presentation, environmental projection, social media integration, oh my! Do we even know how to have a service without electricity anymore? One would hope but there is no doubt that churches have fully embraced technology as aids to the worship service experience, even in traditional settings as well. Now I'm a huge fan of what technology can do to help share the gospel of Jesus Christ. But I know that technology is only a positive influence when it is utilized well in a way that reinforces worship and isn't a distraction. Whether you have cutting edge haze machines or moving lights or are still only using Powerpoint for lyrics (come on, it's the 21st century already, really…Powerpoint?!), one reality faces all of us as lead worshippers, we're using tech, we're probably responsible for it, and we need actual people to run it who know what they're doing.

Most churches these days tend to put the responsibility of manning and maintaining their A/V under the oversight of the Worship Pastor or Worship Director which means it's likely going to fall to you make sure everything runs smoothly. This means you'll be overseeing your church's Production Team. It has been my experience that this is a ministry area where a great number of young or inexperienced worship leaders make the most mistakes. Most churches and even most worship leaders tend to treat their Production Teams with either benign neglect or outright contempt. Production Teams tend to be the red-headed stepchild of ministry and quite honestly, it's a terrible shame. I've witnessed first-hand the animosity that can exist between those who run the production booth and those on the platform. There is a prevalent "us versus them" culture that runs rampant in a number of churches I've encountered, and it leads to division, resentment, and people leaving the church. This is largely because the two groups are often not treated equally and its usually the Production Team that the ends up getting the short straw. Not to mention they tend to be overworked and vastly underappreciated. This results in a Production Team that tends to not be resourced with people or equipment, excluded from discipleship efforts, and downright excluded from ministry time altogether. My hope is to show a better way of organizing and running a Production Team that flourishes and is a critical asset to the mission of executing worship services with excellence.

Bringing Production In

I'm going to venture to say that as a worship leader, you are likely a musician. That being said, you aren't going to have to be very intentional at all about spending time with and working with the other members of your team who are on the platform with you. You *will* have to be exceedingly intentional about investing in your Production Team. I encourage you to make the decision right now to consider your Production Team as worship leaders, too. This is a matter of team culture. Don't believe me that they're worship leaders? Imagine an empty sound or production booth during a service. How good is your service with no one to EQ sound, or advance lyrics slides or put the pastor's scripture reference on the screen, or even turn the lights on? You may be thinking that sounds like your team right now. Now imagine a fully staffed Production Team with everyone doing the jobs right and making everyone on the platform shine for the glory of God during worship. Your Production people have a tremendous impact on whether you're making a joyful noise or whether you're just an obnoxious clanging cymbal. They have an integral role leading your people to the throne room every time you have service as a church. They are worship leaders and it's time you start treating them that way if you aren't already. Just remember, they can shut your mic off anytime they want, you want to love them and make sure they know it. Seriously though, the first thing you need to do if you want an awesome Production Team is change the culture to where the Production Team is a co-equal branch of your ministry. Bring them into the fold of the Worship Arts Team. This means you must be passionate about investing in them, developing systems that build excellence among them, and cultivating leadership within the team.

An absolute must to achieve this is to require your Production Team be present. We require our Production Team to be a part of rehearsals in our ministry. When I first considered making this requirement years ago, I was honestly scared of the ramifications that might occur. To my delight, instead of revolt, I got gratitude. Our Production Team members take part in all aspects of our preparation, which means they are a part of the family, and they love it. They're not on the fringes, they're fully engaged in the ministry, but this only happens because they are there when we study scripture. They're there when we discuss the scriptural basis for a song. They're there when we pray for someone on the team. This inclusion builds a family as well as functional understanding of what we are trying to accomplish through music and A/V. This harmony results in team members working together to produce the best sound or the best lighting look because we all know we are loved by the entire team and are working together to accomplish the same mission. Our team often witnesses Platform Team members deferring to the needs of Production Team needs in matters of staging or EQ. When was the last time one of your singers acted like this? Hopefully they are but if they're not ask yourself why? Our platform folks know they're being asked to do certain things because the Production Team wants to make their efforts even better. This only happens because we spend the time together investing in one another and ministering to one another. We know we all have each other's best interests at heart and want everyone to succeed so that the ministry can succeed. Rehearsals are required for everyone and that means Production Team people as well. Now this is the group that tends to fight this requirement the most because they don't necessarily see themselves as performers and may not initially grasp the need to be at a rehearsal. You may have to be firm with this team regarding this policy but believe me its worth it. It is the foundation upon which all the success of your Production Team rests.

Training and Cross-Training

Now that you've reorganized your Production Team as a central piece of your Worship Arts Ministry, let's talk about turning Production Team prospects into team members. Just as you should have an Audition Process for prospects who sign up to be your musicians, you should have a Training Process for people interested in serving with A/V. Don't forget in your recruiting efforts to mention this aspect of the Worship Arts Team so that you're getting prospects for the Production Team and not just musicians.

It is probably safe to assume that almost no one who initially volunteers to work with A/V in the church knows what they're doing. Now don't get me wrong, you may have people show up who have experience with A/V, but not *your* A/V. They may know sound design but they don't know your digital console and they certainly don't know the *way* your ministry uses the tech you have. It is abundantly important that you spend time providing training for Production Team members. What you absolutely cannot do is expect people to operate something the first time they show up.

My father-in-law is a great guy. He's a believer and a faithful church attender. He's a very generous man and always has a great story with a funny punchline that gets better every time he tells it. He's usually quick to help which is why it's no surprise he decided to volunteer a while back to help with A/V at his church. Now my father-in-law, Robert, isn't a tech wiz but he can handle himself with a computer or a smart phone; he's a capable guy. The church he volunteered for had him arrive thirty minutes early before church the next week so they could "show him some things". Showing him some things consisted of one person giving him about fifteen minutes of a walkthrough on how to use the presentation software they were using (which are seldom simple pieces of software) and then the person had to leave and left Robert to run the worship service that morning. My father-in-law promptly never returned to help his church with this ministry ever again. He was so uncomfortable and so flustered by the time Sunday was over he was scared off from ever helping with production ever again. The church had failed to equip my father-in-law and set him up to succeed or at the very least feel comfortable and enjoy serving in this vital ministry in the church.

This story conveys how critical it is that we provide training for people who sign up to serve in Production. If your people are scared or stressed out, you're failing them, and they won't stick around. Care for your people enough to give them a comfort level with the technology and operating procedures of your church before tossing them in the deep end of Production ministry. Let me tell you what our team does to accomplish this.

Training starts at Rehearsal, and we operate on the assumption that no one knows how to do anything. Training begins at square one for everyone. If someone has some experience that's great, that just means they'll progress through training quickly. New prospects start attending rehearsal and are scheduled via Planning Center just like the rest of our team. Rehearsal really is the best place to see equipment in action, learn operating procedures, and catch team culture. It also provides adequate time for instruction, questions, shadowing, and feedback. I'll lay out our process for training new production team volunteers in the Chapter 12 – Technical Difficulties. At the end of Rehearsal the first week, I like to ask the trainee how they felt about things and whether they want to continue training or if they want to back out. The first week of training doubles as a Test Drive for Production Team. This allows people who feel overwhelmed to back out early rather than late in the process or once they're on the team. If they're still excited about Production Team, then I will send them home with the Worship Arts Team Orientation Packet. By week two they start doing some of the prep work we do in rehearsals like programming lights or setting up video shots. The point is to get them hands on with the gear but not necessarily run a position during services. By the third week they are prepping and running with a veteran team member looking over their shoulder as they go. After that it's up to the Production Leadership Team and the trainee to decide whether someone is ready to go to be released to serve on their own or if they need or want more time. Just like with our musicians, we never rush someone to serve on their own, we let them tell us when they're comfortable and feel qualified to operate on their own. Once they're trained and the Production Director signs off, we add to our tracking document that someone is qualified for a particular position. Then, once they get the Covenant signed and returned, they're eligible to be scheduled to serve.

We will also schedule standalone sessions outside of rehearsal times for training team members if we implement a new piece of technology. When we add something new or make a large change to how we operate we try to train the whole team so everyone is aware and then the team can discuss any unforeseen consequences to all Production roles as a result of the addition or change. This session also provides time to let everyone get hands-on with new gear without the time constraints of rehearsal or services.

We also place a high priority on cross-training. There is not a church in the world that ever has enough volunteers. Jesus said "The harvest is plenty, but the laborers are few." (Luke 10:2) Because of this reality its crucial to have multiple people who can operate different positions. Whether it's because you rotate team volunteers or you end up with someone who must drop out for some reason, you never want to be dependent on one person to keep you afloat. We absolutely believe in having people operate in their strengths, but we also know the value of having people be capable of shifting around to fill critical gaps in the team at a moment's notice. This means we intentionally schedule current team members for weeks of training where they can learn a new position. This means your team bench must have depth to accomplish this but keep building the team and your numbers will get to the point where you can support this practice. This means we have team members in our Training Tracking document who are qualified to serve in multiple positions. It is also a requirement for us that anyone who wants to serve as a Sunday Producer must be qualified in most if not all the positions that we have in our Production Team. This ensures consistent quality each week regardless of who's serving in which position because the Sunday Producer knows each position well and how to help others as they serve in those roles. A Sunday Producer is a critical role you will want to have as a part of your Production Team.

The Sunday Producer

While there are many possible roles for a Production Team, there is one role you absolutely can't do without if you want a top-notch Production Team for your church and that's the Sunday Producer. A Sunday Producer has a few primary, critical roles. In the midst of a worship service, their primary role is to ensure the accurate and timely flow of a worship service. This means calling out cues, following the service schedule, and troubleshooting any technical issues that may arise. This role oversees the rest of the Production Team in the Production Booth but ideally doesn't handle any of the operating roles. This frees them up to help anyone who may have an issue and interact with any stagehands you may have on your team or other Production Team members who may not perform their role in the Production Booth. Their job is to be the connective tissue of all the production aspects of your service. They keep things flowing and keep things working. They also serve as spiritual leader by leading prayer for the Production Team each week and helping to build disciples among the team. In rehearsals their job is to oversee training, fill any gaps in volunteers, ensure effective preparation for services, troubleshoot A/V issues, and to be the bridge of communication between the Production Team and you the Worship Pastor and members of the Platform Team as needed. Teach your Platform Team to communicate to you or the Production Director instead of having all your musicians constantly shouting at people in the booth. Your Production Team members will thank you and communication will be better amongst your team. My Sunday Producers also tend to be part of our Leadership Team of our Worship Arts Team. Their insight in making our worship services better has been invaluable through the years.

Our Production Team culture and training system has led to better prospect retention and team member longevity. Our people feel part of our team and are committed to fulfilling the mission of our church and ministry. We never have enough people, but we are consistently well staffed and the quality of our Production and A/V elements demonstrate the effectiveness of our approach.

I thought I would include a list of all the Production Roles we have utilized at our services just for your knowledge as you build your team:

- ➢ Production Director (Paid Staff)
- ➢ Sunday Producer
- ➢ House Sound Engineer
- ➢ Recording and Streaming Sound Engineer
- ➢ Computer Presentation
- ➢ Lighting Design
- ➢ Video Producer
- ➢ Robotic Camera Operator
- ➢ Camera Operator
- ➢ Platform Manager
- ➢ Platform Hand
- ➢ Spot Light Operator
- ➢ Photographer/Historian

8 – Building the Dream Team

He makes the whole body fit together perfectly. As each part does its own special work, it helps the other parts grow, so that the whole body is healthy and growing and full of love.

Ephesians 4:16 NLT

Building teams is hard work. Building a healthy team that functions at a high-capacity level over a long time, is full of people who are committed to the team mission and are loyal and dependable is the dream of any leader or manager. Team building is often messy work because it involves the human element. The human element requires leaders to develop systems that unleash the talents and passions of team members in a way that serves the interest of the organization and meets the needs of the team members at the same time. The human element also requires leaders to be sensitive to the uniqueness of each member of the whole and yet place a high priority on a vision that surpasses the importance of any one individual. Sounds like ministry doesn't it. The reality is that building a worship team is no different than building any other team. At the same time, a worship ministry has its own unique nature and building the team to run this ministry can prove challenging. Most, but not all, ministry teams do not require a lot of advanced preparation on the part of team volunteers. In this way worship ministry is very unique. Worship ministry requires practice at home and rehearsals prior to serving. Most ministries don't absolutely need their team members operating in sync with one another. Music ministry obviously makes this a necessity. In order to meet these types of unique challenges that worship ministries face we have to be dedicated to intentional team building and crafting the culture of the team that specifically pertains to worship teams.

The ideal is to have a team that shows up prepared and ready to give their all to serve God's church from a completely selfless heart condition. The unique nature of the arts and the extra requirements needed to produce polished worship services week in and week out means that the requirements upon team members should be unapologetically different and elevated. Any worship leader must take great care to be intentional about building a team that takes seriously the responsibility of leading worship in the local church. This is the work of building a specific team culture. Culture is the common values that either enable teams to unify to work together as one towards a vision or mires a team in disunity, conflict, and ultimately ineffectiveness for the Lord. That last phrase should make you shudder. The principles I wish to present in this chapter have proven over time to produce these desired results of worship team unity and empowerment and insulate your team from the conflict that arises from people not all being on the same page. My hope is that the strategies laid out in this chapter will prove fruitful in your own setting and as you read ahead think about whether you have implemented any of these approaches already, and if you haven't, how would these team and culture building strategies look if applied to your ministry.

Disciple the Lifestyle

If you have ever travelled anywhere of note in the world, you've likely taken a tour to see the sights, especially if it's a major tourist location that you've never been before. I'm willing to bet you didn't just ride or walk around and look at things with no guidance or someone to point out noteworthy places. I'm talking about a tour guide or at least a good YELP review. Someone who has lived in the location, knows its history, can point to places where great moments of history have taken place or highlight unique and amazing architecture. How much more interesting and vibrant a city or landscape becomes when someone can point the way to the things, sights, sounds, tastes, and smells that really matter.

Isn't that what a worship leader should be? Shouldn't a worship leader be the one who has already been to the mountain top or smelled the aroma of the Holy Spirit or tasted the freedom of grace? Shouldn't a worship leader be pointing the way to what really matters in the presence of God? How can anyone hope to accomplish this if they are a tourist with no experience of God in their lives? Worship leaders have to involve themselves with God's kingdom in more ways than practice, rehearsal, and services. Worship leaders must lead the charge in their families and in their church by living a lifestyle of worship.

This concept goes back to the earlier chapter on worship theology and how our worship under the New Covenant established by Christ is to be worship through every waking moment of our lives. This brings us back to our discussion of Romans 12. It is not enough for worship leaders to show up to worship, but rather leading in a service has to be the point in a worship leader's life where they take brothers and sisters in Christ to spiritual places they have *already* been. It is not a moment of worship but rather an aspect of their ongoing and never-ending worship.

For my worship team, this is the single most important aspect of discipleship that we focus on. Anyone who joins the team is constantly encouraged to engage in worship every day and all day as a lifestyle. When our team members are worshipping God constantly, growth and discipleship are built into their lives. I don't have to design fancy discipleship programs or training programs or even establish protections for our team for those who aren't spiritually mature enough. The understanding is that everyone is at different points in the discipleship journey but also growth is explicitly expected. When we are focused on teaching our team members to live lives of worship it is apparent that no one is perfect in that pursuit and that we all strive to be more devoted to worshipping our Lord non-stop. Our team discussions focus on how our lives either do or don't reflect that we are living lives as acts of worship and how we can do better. It is important in these times that you insist upon people talking and sharing specifics in their life. This is not a time for theory, this is a time for authenticity and real life.

Having our team members focus their growth on living lives of worship translates into them being better worship leaders. They can encourage people to follow where they have already been. And I'm not talking about "worshipping" better because they know our worship songs better from practicing more on their own. They can sing, play, and praise in worship services through experience because they are constantly wrestling with pursuing sanctification and more easily identify with growth and success, battles and struggle, brokenness and victory. Their worship becomes exceedingly more like personal testimonies and less like creative storytelling. This has a profound impact on the level of authenticity in the corporate worship environment, something we all struggle with and strive to achieve a deeper level of as worship team leaders.

Most discipleship efforts with regards to lifestyle worship have to do with submitting to God's will instead of our own. Submission and deferring to what is Godly is a large part of what you will need to discuss, study in God's Word, and model for your team. And modeling lifestyle worship has to be consistent both when your team is gathered and when they are not gathered. You'll want to be looking for moments of lifestyle worship among your team that you can celebrate as a team and point to as ideals for people to emulate. Whenever you talk about lifestyle worship remember to always connect the dots between personal worship and leading others in worship and how the two are not separate but rather two expressions of the same pursuit of discipleship and being like Jesus. It is also very important to find other ways to serve the local church and the community at large as a team. This might be bringing music to some event, but it may also be physical work at some church event or mission project. This helps to reinforce that worship is a lifestyle and not opportunities for performance.

You will likely also find that making lifestyle worship the main focus of the discipleship efforts of your worship team will pay added dividends. When the focus is constantly making Jesus famous, always praising Him, and deferring to His will for our lives, you will find your people are more team-ministry minded. Their focus is Kingdom first and self last. This helps protect your team members from falling into the traps of being divas or needing the spotlight to show off their talents. You'll discover your team celebrates each other's successes rather than trying to compete for their time to be the star. When the point of your worship team is pointing your church's people to Jesus and taking people to God's throne where your team has been all week in their lives, they will demand people focus on them as talented musicians less and less. This also helps people roll with setbacks (like a mic not working, or messing up lyrics, or crucifying that guitar lead line) in rehearsals and services more because they don't need to look good. Your people know the point is not about them but rather bringing glory and honor to God and encouraging and challenging others in service to do the same. When Jesus has been the star in their lives all week, they will want others to see Jesus as the star during rehearsal and service gatherings. At the end of the day, you should discover your team has a very healthy foundation from which to operate together where Jesus comes first in all things and individual needs are secondary to ministry objectives and needs.

Insist on High Accountability - The Worship Arts Team Orientation Packet

Part of your role as a worship pastor or worship leader in the local church is to be one of the greatest champions for excellence in your church's worship service. We are called to give our very best to God and "work as unto the Lord" (Colossians 3). In my opinion, excellence does not happen by accident. Greatness can flash in a moment from anyone, anywhere, but excellence, especially when related to teamwork and ministry, must be systematic. God can do amazing things in spite of our lousy efforts, but we are more faithful servants when we intentionally do the work of planning and implementation of the efforts for His kingdom. I also believe that true excellence is measured over the long term and not in the immediate. Excellence goes hand in hand with consistency. As long as there is someone who does not call Jesus Lord then there is still work to be done as His followers and we must continually give our very best to win souls so no one is left without a loving relationship with the Father and the eternal life that is promised.

This means that there must be standards and benchmarks for what we define as excellence on our team, and we must ensure our team members know what these standards are. We must define the "win", outline the strategies for achieving and maintaining excellence, and insist that our team members uphold these standards. This is how we craft our team culture. We tell our team members what our ideals are, and we describe what will be celebrated and what won't be tolerated in order to achieve the team's ministry mission. This facet of team building lays the groundwork that enables every team to be on the same page. When team expectations and guidelines are communicated clearly and upfront, it removes a lot of the guesswork of what is expected of your team members and ensures that the standards for excellence are adhered to.

When it comes to my worship ministry this is largely accomplished through our Worship Arts Team Orientation Packet. This document is given to each and every one of our Platform Team and Production Team members when they first come on the team. The packet is certainly not exhaustive, but it is thorough. We pack a lot of information into our packet so we give our team members some time to take it home and read through it at their pace and ask any questions that may arise. The following is a topical breakdown of what is included in our WAT Orientation Packet:

- Worship Theology – We want all of our people to know why we do what we do, for whom we do it, and who we're doing it with.

- Living For Excellence – This is our chance to communicate our team culture, lifestyle worship, and being a good citizen of God's church.
- Becoming a Servant Leader – This section describes the ideal heart of someone who serves on the Worship Team and encourages new team members to adopt this heart condition.
- Sharing My Life With Others – We communicate the importance of community and evangelism both personally, within the church body, and in the world at large.
- Giving of Our Time, Treasure, and Talent – this section seeks to reinforce our church vision for giving and also teaches that our talents and resources are gifts that are supposed to benefit the church, not ourselves.
- Team Attendance Requirements – We very clearly lay out what our requirements are for rehearsals and services. We require attendance at rehearsal for the weeks people are scheduled to serve. If someone can't attend rehearsal, they are not allowed on the platform Sunday, and we communicate that in this section.
- "LAUNCH" Guide – "LAUNCH" is our Bible Study and Prayer time that we share at each Rehearsal. Our team members are required to periodically prepare our "LAUNCH" and we lay out what we would like them to prepare and how. This time may look different on your team, but the idea is to communicate your expectations for study and growth as a member of the team.

- Some Things You Will Need to Know to Be Prepared – Here we discuss some various team policies and some available resources and tools we use to prepare for rehearsals and services.
- Your Influence Off the Platform – This section describes the importance of a worship leader's witness off of the platform and how to live lives worthy of the special privilege of being a visible leader in the church as a worship leader.
- How To Prepare For Your Next Rehearsal – This sections speaks directly to our musicians and gives them tips for how to best practice music throughout the week.
- 10 Things You Need To Know About Sundays – This sections describes some things to be prepared for in terms of scheduling and mental preparedness for serving for a full Sunday. Our church has multiple services and there are some dynamics that impact our team since we serve all day that we want our team members prepared for.
- Where You Fit In – We give our Worship Team Members our Organizational Chart to look at. I want our team members to know how they fit into to the larger effort of preparing worship and doing the work of God's Kingdom in our specific church. I strongly feel this helps cut down on competition and animosity between our Platform Team and Production Team as our team members see right upfront that they are peers working on the same team and should seek to serve each other as we prepare and work together.

- Worship Arts Team Covenant – This page is a page that summarizes all the standards the new team member just read and asks them to sign and return the Covenant to our leadership team. A signature means team members understand our team expectations, guidelines, and definition of excellence and they agree to uphold the standards and also agree to help hold other team members accountable.

No one serves on our Worship Arts Team without reading the Orientation Packet and signing the Covenant. There was a time when I oversaw worship ministry and had *none* of these standards in place. I will tell you firsthand that I can look back on those days and I get a little nauseous. I wish I could describe for you the chaos that was our rehearsals and long-term ministry outlook but that's probably a matter for a different kind of book. Not to mention the interpersonal difficulties I faced with my team members. We weren't operating with the same baseline. We all had different motivations, different agendas, different ideas of what our success looked like and I'm not kidding when I say that when people have different ideas of what success and excellence look like on a worship team, conflict is inevitable. Not because we are bad people but because we care about our craft so deeply, it's who we are as artists.

I received some good coaching from a fellow worship leader along the way and he was insistent upon implementing some basic team expectations. He knew from experience how doing so elevated his worship team to astounding heights. The expectations he described sounded good for his team, but I was terrified to even require attendance at rehearsal because I had convinced myself that people would either rebel or not be able to live up to the commitment I asked of them. But I felt God calling my ministry to greater devotion and greater levels of preparation and I eventually became convicted I needed to step out in faith and implement a number of excellence standards. To my surprise, I didn't lose a single team member and in fact had several team members thank me for making their investment in the team more worthwhile. They were waiting for me to turn our ministry into something valuable and worth spending their time doing. For them to comment in this way, I took it as they saw me as not valuing them by not expecting more. It was then that I realized how important things like mission and purpose and accountability are when it comes to getting people to buy into what a team is trying to accomplish. Setting the bar higher and not apologizing for it in reality builds commitment and participation on a team rather than scaring people off. I think many Christian leaders are afraid to set high standards for ministry teams because they are afraid of chasing away people, but my experience has shown over and over that high accountability brings people into the team with greater intensity. It conveys that what you are trying to accomplish is vitally important and worth ensuring that the team is effective. After all, isn't the work of Jesus's church the most important work we can be engaged in?

I have witnessed people become almost heartbroken over coming up short against our standards for excellence, not because they are afraid of repercussions from me or our leadership team, but because they have bought in to the vision for excellence and want to make sure they are helping contribute to that aim. They will occasionally feel disappointed in themselves for not upholding the standards they agreed to. It is certainly not my aim to make anyone feel bad, but I do love seeing my people care so much about our team. It demonstrates their dedication. Which also leads to my one caution when it comes to implementing these kinds of standards and strategies.

Underneath the high bar needs to be a whole lot of grace and leeway. Our team standards for excellence should be a guide and a benchmark for ideals. They should never be a measuring stick for a person's worth and value. They should also not be used to shame people who don't measure up. In ministry, people always come first, especially over some contrived piece of paper and set of rules. Thanks to our packet and Covenant, our people know our expectations and will largely police themselves and each other. But when something comes up and someone can't make a rehearsal due to a family illness, or someone shows up and didn't practice their music because their job has been insane lately, we show grace, never legalism. We always work with people to try and find compromises and ways to help get them prepared and ready if possible. At the same time, we use our standards for excellence to challenge people to take the next step spiritually or technically. We give people something higher to stretch for and spur them towards growth. And we're not afraid to rely on the standards to challenge people in love to strive for something better.

I've also found people will remove *themselves* when they can't meet their commitments. This has saved me so many difficult conversations because I seldom must ask someone to step down for not abiding by the Covenant. Usually, they know they are falling short and will either correct their habits or step down from the team. Either way the team is made stronger and healthier, and I didn't have to be the bad guy. When I have had to address issues, the Covenant being in place gives me a firm footing for addressing unwanted or ungodly behaviors and gives me something to point to that they signed and agreed to. It's a much better conversation when you call someone on something when they said they would abide by a prearranged agreement. This gives your leadership some protection and your ministry added credibility. This means, however, that you must become comfortable letting go of the few folks who just aren't wired to live up to your ministry's expectations. While we should do our very best to include as many people as possible in the work of ministry, the unique nature of worship ministry and what it takes to have excellent offerings of worship means that not everyone will be able to make the cut. Some people just won't be a fit in your culture but that's ok, God still has a plan for their life and your team will be healthier because you don't have a worship team made up of flaky people.

The culture of excellence starts with the Orientation Packet, but it must be *reinforced* consistently over time. It is not enough to tell your people one time where the target of excellence is. It must be woven into your team's gatherings regularly. Once or twice each year I will take the team through the entire Packet or at least hit points that need addressing. Also, when addressing individual circumstances that come up you should always reference your team's packet and Covenant as to why you're making some critical decision or even when making exceptions. Exceptions demonstrate you're a leader that has a capacity for grace. Be sure to communicate exceptions to your team and why you've made them. You don't want your exceptions to lead to feelings from other team members of resentment for someone not abiding by your teams' standards and getting away with it. It helps teach and it helps reinforce important aspects of team culture and expectations and it helps prevent accusations of favoritism. Reinforcement leads to habits which become trends; trends become culture. It prevents you from creating moving targets which can really frustrate volunteers. Most people want to please and do a good job and if that metric constantly changes, your team will get frustrated and not continue to serve. Your team should know without a doubt what is expected and how the team operates to meet those expectations.

This extends to an aspect of team excellence culture that can be difficult to capsulize to but is vitally important to foster. To really cement team culture, it is crucial that you have a team that is capable of and expected to teach others the team culture. You must make sure that you have a *teaching team*. If your team can't relay the important aspects of why and how your ministry does what it does to others, then it should be pretty obvious that your team is not as unified as it should be. There is no greater method of learning something than having to teach something. For our team, this means we pair new people with team veterans for the first few weeks. Not only does this help people get up to speed faster with technical details for getting ready for our services but it also ensures that new team members are immersed in our culture immediately. Our team members know it is their job to help answer questions and provide guidance as someone adjusts to serving on our team. This helps new people pick up on what we think is important, but it also helps our veterans stay fresh on our standards. I can't overstate how much having a teaching team protects against wandering from our mission and core values because they are always in the forefront of our collective team interactions. And this is also why the effort can be difficult to capsulize and replicate. This really is very organic. How and what each team member communicates will be different week to week, team member to team member. I personally feel that it is the expectation to be a teaching team that is most critical and not necessarily the how. Like I said, we tend to use the buddy system for someone's first few weeks, but

I am sure there are other ways you could have your team be engaged in teaching and re-teaching your team's standards for excellence. It may take some time for this to be fruitful in your ministry but when the concept grabs hold, your team culture will become deep rooted and hard to shake. Mission focus runs deep, and team health and effectiveness tend to elevate.

Take the Bullet Whenever You Possibly Can

In all of my years of worship ministry the number of people on my worship ministry team that were professional musicians, someone who's job was to make or teach music as daily profession and got paid has been low, a handful at most out of hundreds. As well, I can only recall *ever* one person who was actually a professional in the world of production, she worked for a local TV station as producer. Now you may be fortunate enough to work for a church where these numbers are better but I'm willing to assume that most church worship teams are comprised largely of unpaid volunteers who aren't professionals in the performing or visual arts industries. This means we serve alongside volunteers who have passion and maybe a calling but lack training and experience in the arts in a professional environment. Even with the best training, coaching, and other talent around them they will inevitably make mistakes in their technical craft in the midst of your rehearsals and worship services.

In addition, your volunteers overall are likely lay members of the church. They're not going to be pastors, ministers, theologians, or counselors. This means they are likely not people who live in the full image of Christ. *No one* is for sure, and your people are in all different places on the spiritual journey toward being like Jesus. This means they are going to make social, moral, and emotional mistakes because "all have sinned and fall short of the glory of God." (Romans 3:23) And you are their shepherd. And they are your sheep. It is your job to protect them, even if they get themselves into a sheep mess. In terms of team building, this means you as a leader should be known by your team as someone who takes a bullet for your team members. And there will be lots of bullets to go around.

When my wife and I were in our twenties, she served as an intern for the youth ministry at the church we were attending. A trip had been planned for some of the youth that had excelled in the past year serving in the church and in the community. The trip was intended to be a reward and was slated as a few days in Key West enjoying the beach and seeing some sights. To make a long story short, the trip didn't go well, and some parents of the youth were upset at events that had transpired on the trip. The most "egregious" being the youth were given alcohol-free strawberry daquiris one day while hanging out on the beach. What was intended as fun by trip leaders was taken as inappropriate by parents. I don't know your position on alcohol, but it was received as imitating giving kids alcohol. In the days that followed the church leadership, senior and youth pastors, proceeded to lay the blame on my wife rather than own their own decisions. This left my wife feeling betrayed and hung out to dry and left alone to face the anger and wrath of the parents. Let's just say it was the beginning of the end of our time attending that church…at all.

There's a saying that "everyone has a boss" and it's true. We all report to someone. Even CEO's report to boards and elected officials report to their constituencies. If you've ever experienced a situation where someone who supervises you doesn't have your back and tries to shift blame for a mistake to you as a subordinate, you know how much that hurts and how frustrating the situation can be. You feel abused, expendable, and undervalued. There is an innate sense in most of us that those we report to should also defend us and protect us from attack, not throw us under the bus. You may have also experienced a time when you genuinely have made a mistake but have had the support of your supervisor regardless. In one case all trust in your leader is lost, in the other you feel more endeared to your leader and to the organization they represent. It is also important to consider the statistical trend that people quit their boss, not their job. People will tolerate incredibly terrible work if they know the person above them values them, appreciates them, and goes to bat for them in difficult times. Conversely, people will leave amazing, dream jobs with outstanding benefit packages because of a single person, their boss. Many studies and surveys convey the reality that a majority of workers leave employment positions because of their boss and not because their work or actual job tasks. All of this speaks to the principle that you as ministry leader will need to own a lot of short-comings and mistakes.

Ultimately, you are in command and if one of your people screws something up the best thing you can do is be an advocate for your people and to own as much of a situation as you can. If your goal is to build a team both numerically and spiritually then this is one of the greatest contributing factors to building confidence in your leadership in worship ministry. Worship services have lots of moving pieces, most of which revolve around some aspect of the arts. The arts often involve taking some risks to explore ideas and emotions. Not to mention our worship services nowadays are filled with cutting edge technology that can go haywire with the touch of a single button. Ministry also can't happen without people and people are just plain messy. Their lives are imperfect and hectic, and people are going to make decisions that fall short of God's will and will have an impact on the influence of your ministry. It is in these moments that you can either be more concerned about your own pride, prestige, and job security or you can be more concerned about caring for people and protecting them from as much hurt and strife as possible. This means you will need to claim ownership when the lyric slides aren't in the right order. This means you'll need to be prepared to step in and vouch for someone's character when they've stepped on someone else's toes. This means you'll need to own your call to have someone sing a solo and they bomb. This doesn't mean you need to make excuses for people or lie to cover things up but you can take these moments and decide to be proactive and teach your people where they can be better and not throw them under the bus at the same time. This also means standing in the way of the flaming arrows from other people in your church who are quick to be critical. You wanted to be in charge remember, well as the old saying goes...the buck stops with you. A team's shortcomings aren't your shortcomings, but they are your responsibility to improve and its vitally important to improve the efforts while at the same time making sure your people are uplifted and encouraged, not blown up and cast aside. It your job to field as much criticism as possible with as much grace as possible all while sparing your team members the harsh feedback of others. It is then your responsibility to walk alongside your team members and coach them up to be better artists and better ministry leaders within your church. Be an aide in helping God take what is meant for evil and turn it for good.

When you are known as a leader who will take a bullet you should see two aspects of your team improve. The first is team morale should elevate. If your people aren't constantly being bombarded with feedback about shortcomings, they can focus more on their successes. Having a positive outlook always translates into more efficient and effective teams. A positive outlook encourages further creativity and the feeling of freedom to pursue ideas and reach for higher heights. The importance of team confidence can't be understated with respect to those who serve on the platform. Trust me, you don't want a team full of worship leaders with no confidence because they are only constantly reminded of their flaws. Building an infectious worship spirit from the platform requires leaders who are bold and feel comfortable putting themselves out front for others to follow in worship abandon.

The other aspect of your team that you should witness improve is team loyalty and commitment. When your team knows you have their back, they know their presence is valued and they are in a safe place. We all want to feel safe and protected in life. Your people will be more committed to the ministry because they know their leader looks out for them. You, as leader, reflect God's mercy, protection, and grace which spurs your people on to serve His causes with greater zeal. These moments where you step in the way of someone else's bullet can be some of the most trying times in ministry and often not really fair to you, but these are those times where you must lay down your own ego because you are there to serve and not be served. A leader who takes someone else's bullet will produce more confident and committed team members.

Volunteers Are Like Cats

I am a cat person. Now don't get me wrong, I don't have any problems with dogs or dog people. For a long stretch of my young life, I really wanted to be a veterinarian when I grew up. I love all kinds of animals but when it comes to companions at home, I'm a cat person. They really are fun little creatures of God and I have had several in my life that I truly consider some of the best friends I've ever had. There was a stretch in my career where I worked from home because the church that I was serving at the time was launched in a school so we didn't have (and couldn't afford) a central church office. One of my cats at the time, Dothan, went to work with me every day. As I sat in my office all those years working at my desk, he would sit on the back of my office chair and "help". Most of the time he would nap but he would also decide to chase his tail on the back of my office chair. Yes, on the back of the chair. It was really something to watch him spin these tight circles over and over on the back of my chair. You may laugh but if you've had a work from home job you may understand how valuable his companionship was. Working from home can be pretty lonely in fact. I had cats growing up and my family has several to this day. In all the years I've had cats living in my house there is one truth that I have learned when it comes to cats.

Cats don't take orders.

Cats can be very loving and playful. Cats can be amazing pets, friends, and companions. Cats can even play very skillfully and be a joy to watch and play with. But cats don't take orders. You can coax cats to perform tricks or stunts and most of the time they might oblige but the moment you try to command a cat, they ignore you. You can yell at a cat, but it will likely scare off. But when you try to demand that a cat do something you want it to, it won't listen and will likely turn around, walk away, and show you its backside as it goes. One must earn a cat's love and cooperation. Unlike dogs that can be trained and will faithfully obey orders, cats require incentive and trust. Blind obedience is pretty rare for a cat.

Volunteers are like cats. When you are organizing and leading your team you must always be mindful of the fact that your people are volunteers and thus are choosing to be present. You must treat them as such. You can't throw your weight around barking orders and hope your people will tolerate that for very long. When you are engaged in ministry with your worship team you must seek to build trust and rapport with your people. You must always be pointing back to the "why's" of your church and ministry. You can't assume people will always stay bought in to what you are trying to accomplish and blindly follow along and do what you say. You must also make sure that your team culture values team involvement with strategy and planning. You can't be the "worship dictator" and expect people to care about the ministry when they have no voice and no skin in the game. We'll get to some ways on how to ensure you are getting team input in your ministry later in this chapter and in future chapters as well. This concept really is vital to any ministry in the church but let me share with you a worship ministry specific example.

A few years ago, the church where I'm currently serving decided to host a regional men's conference. My team was tasked with running Production for the entire event and lead several sessions of corporate worship during the event. The event was held in a space on our campus that our church adults are not used to worshipping in, our Student Building. The building was previously the church's sanctuary and was built in the late 1980's. The acoustics are pretty terrible and not at all suited for modern worship music and a full band but I didn't have say over the venue so we did the best we could with the environment. To compound our difficulties, when we arrived for sound check on the first evening of the conference, all of the settings in our sound console that had been saved from our rehearsal earlier in the week had somehow been lost. We had to re-EQ *everything*. As we were working through the issues and people were arriving for the event, one of the leaders of the event felt that the volume in the space was too loud and started making demands to my production team to reduce the volume level. What the event leader wasn't aware of was the technical problems we were experiencing and the nature of the acoustics of the space. You see the old sanctuary is one of those venues where human bodies soak up a ton of the volume once people are in place. My team knew this and were prepared ahead of time, but the event leader's demands came anyway. Our church is also right beside Ft. Liberty (formerly Ft. Bragg) and most of our people are soldiers for the U.S. Army. This means we have lots of people accustomed to chain of command and giving and taking orders. And yet, my production team, comprised almost entirely of army soldiers, was on the verge of mutiny and were threatening to leave the event because of the treatment they felt they were receiving. You see, even these group of guys who are accustomed to following orders were ready to turn around, walk away, and show us their backsides on the way out because someone barked an order at them at church. Chain of command doesn't extend off post to our church campus. If *soldiers* don't take orders at my church, average people certainly won't take orders at your church, at least not often and not for long before they quit. Our event leader thought he was facing dogs, and instead was facing cats. It took a significant amount of my time and focus that night to cool things off and get the conference kicked off, and we got there but the experience had a lasting impact with my production team for some time.

On another occasion I was fortunate to be asked to be guest worship leader in my hometown of Gainesville, FL. The usual part-time worship leader was there and was facilitating the rehearsal with his worship team backing me up musically. The entire night's rehearsal was marked by him stopping songs, barking orders, and people rolling their eyes behind his back. I was familiar with this church and was aware that their worship ministry had not seen a lot of growth in recent years and by the time the night was over I was pretty sure I knew why. The few folks that were present at rehearsal were clearly on their last nerve with this leader. The lack of enthusiasm for his leadership and the culture's direction were palpable. As an outsider it was obvious that this team didn't feel valued, and the team lacked any joy in their work or craft. The negativity also showed when it came time for us all to lead worship that Sunday. There was little enthusiasm from them during worship and it was disheartening to be a member of that worship team for the week. There was great potential and talent there but most of it was squashed by leadership that looked too much like a dictatorship.

I encourage you to see your people as more than resources and instruments to be played. They are people with feelings, desires, agendas, baggage, and potential. Most of your people will also be artists with egos and quirks. You must develop the skill to bring people along with you as you do the Lord's work in worship and not merely make demands of people who don't have to be there. Nothing requires them to stay other than their sense of commitment that they will either feel is being valued and appreciated or taken for granted and taken advantage of. Your people will tire of your directives and will quit coming. You want a team where people feel blessed by coming and want to come back. Build relationships and make big asks, never make demands of your people or bark orders.

Teams That Work...Work

I've spent a large portion of my vocational ministry facilitating worship in environments that weren't designed for contemporary worship styles. I've led in a civil war era church, and I've led in a middle school that we transformed into church week after week. It was only just a few short years ago when my current church built a multi-million-dollar worship center that having a worship service no longer required changing over the venue to meet our needs. All that work was tedious, and I am thankful to have a dedicated contemporary worship space at this point in my life. All that hard work taught me a vital lesson, however. I learned a very important lesson about team building during that time. That lesson was that teams that do actual physical work together are more cohesive teams.

All the years of setting up and tearing down stages, projectors, and sound systems was time spent bonding and building relationships. People grew closer because there was time built into our ministry time for sharing stories and really learning to love one another and really dig around in each others' lives. Some of my best friendships that have come from ministry have been forged in those times working, laughing, building, and crying together. It's important to build into your team time for fun that doesn't involve work, yes, and we will discuss that more in a moment, but I have discovered that fun times can get splintered into cliques and factions whereas physical teamwork tends to be much more focused and unifying. My challenge to you is to find opportunities where your team can work together beyond practicing worship elements. For my team, it was easy for years to have those moments because we had all that gear to set up in our church's gym. It was natural and organic but to this day I still intentionally find ways for my team to all have to pitch in together towards some objective. This might be having them help with a build day on some creative stage design or it sometimes looks like me asking our team members to help prep communion elements. There are some weeks I ask our team to completely rearrange our stage layout. On the one hand I get bored with where things like our drums or piano are placed but as well I know it provides those opportunities for my people to spend some time bonding in the midst of a project (you should ask someone on my team about assembling white Christmas trees sometime). This makes our team tighter which makes our ministry to one another stronger because we are more intimate with the details of each other's lives. I feel strongly that this sense of connection can't help but spill over onto the platform when we worship together. Part of leading worship is creating connection with our church as the body of believers, feeling that sense of belonging. I believe we as worship leaders can help foster this environment by modeling it as we worship together. I am confident that moments are infectious when we worship together, engaging one another on the platform with smiles and celebrating God together as we clap together. And we encourage our people in the rows to join us worshipping together as a family from this attitude. This simply can't happen if we don't have time to spend together without the noise of worship rehearsal. I am confident there are other opportunities around your church where you can get your team involved with some tasks from time to time. Don't fall into the trap of thinking that because people are already there extra with rehearsals that these times aren't needed and valuable. It also helps to continually reinforce that you expect people to be servant leaders in your church in ways beyond being in the spotlight on the platform. These times should be considered as you build a calendar each year. Make sure they are intentionally a part of your year ahead.

I encourage you to look for these opportunities and ask your people to go the second mile.

The Inner Circle

As your team becomes more spiritually mature, effective, efficient, and healthy and as your recruiting efforts begin to bear fruit you will probably begin to notice that your team grows numerically. Healthy teams that produce excellent results are attractive and others will want to join. This also means that you will likely see an increase in the number of leaders within your team as well. All this translates into more people and more moving parts for you to lead and manage. As you continue to develop people and elevate them to leadership positions it will likely be necessary for you to develop something that looks like a leadership team or inner circle to help you. You are one person, and you can't do everything and handle every aspect that your ministry will face. You simply must have other people in place to assist. Here is where I must offer a caution.

Who you allow on your leadership team will become your inner circle in your ministry. And who your inner circle is and how they came to be in the group will profoundly impact your entire ministry. The temptation here is to have people who are the most talented. Or maybe the people on this team are comprised of those who are the most loyal to you and your ministry. Maybe you even have your closest friends in your inner circle. Or maybe it's the most spiritually mature people you can find in your worship ministry. Personally, I think those are all the wrong people to have on your leadership team. So then, who are the right people to have as your right hand people? It's the people who are most bought in to the church's vision and mission and to your worship ministry's vision and mission.

These are the people who will be helping to oversee matters of your team culture when you cannot. You don't want people that are undermining what God has called your ministry to do. You want people who are as big if not bigger champions for the culture of your team.

The important thing here is that you want the most dedicated people in your ministry on your leadership team. Not dedicated to you personally but to the ministry. And don't confuse attendance with dedication. Some of the most dedicated people in ministry can only serve twice a month. But they are a part of my inner leadership team because they work hard for the Lord as a part of our team, I can depend on them, and I know they reinforce our standards for excellence at every turn. This means you will likely have some unexpected people on your leadership team. But you should find these people to be competent to lead because they are sold out on your culture, and they are already deeply invested in your team and your ministries standards and strategies.

It is a great sign of your awesome leadership that you're not afraid to elevate people who aren't necessarily *your* biggest fan but are the ministry's biggest fan. Demonstrate you are able to elevate people who are called and passionate and you don't just play favorites. Remember that as your team grows these people will have a ton of influence on the vibe of your team. My advice is to elevate those that you wish to celebrate as ideal servants and team members. This is a way to celebrate those that have bought in to what God is doing through your worship team and provide examples for people to strive to emulate.

Don't Negotiate a With Hostage Takers

This may be the most gut-wrenching lesson I ever learned in my young years as worship leader. I had been in my first part time paid role for about four months as a worship leader for the church plant I was a part of. Our team was still small and was still mostly made up of the few folks that were there when I came onboard. The team was mostly middle-aged guys who were all excited about music but quite honestly weren't very talented. But still, they seemed to be enthusiastic about the direction of the church and seemed like a group of guys willing to do whatever it took to get the job done.

A couple of the guys also played together in a cover band, and they had frequent gigs around town. Their relationship was pretty tight, and they jived pretty well together as musicians. One of them played bass and sang and the other was a guitarist, lead guitar mostly. He was the only lead guitarist in the entire new church where I found myself, and he knew it. For discussion in this book, we'll call this lead guitarist Jack.

Jack was very intense. He was nice enough most of the time, but he wasn't what anyone would call bubbly. He was very focused on his career, his family, his band, and an amateur hockey team he played for in the area. Jack also brought with him a number of key pieces of equipment each week so that we could have adequate sound for the worship team on Sundays. I assumed that the team sharing his equipment was the way he intended the situation to be, and I never thought twice about changing that status quo. For a couple months everything seemed fine with Jack other than his "schedule" caused him to miss rehearsals a lot and he wasn't the most punctual guy on Sunday mornings.

And then one morning Jack exploded. As was usually the case, my team showed up to setup for services *without* Jack arriving on time. By the time Jack arrived we had almost everything set up and the team was waiting on the equipment Jack brought with him. Once he got to the stage, I asked a couple of the other team members to help grab the equipment and put it into place, the same places they had been used by our team for the few months that I had been there. Jack blew up at me…instantly, and publicly. He was outraged I was "taking" his equipment and refusing to allow him to "use his own stuff". To this day I remember the vein on his forehead throbbing and the one in his neck pulsing as he was yelling at me from the floor below the stage. I was literally shocked and speechless. I had just been going along with what had been taking place before my involvement, but Jack was beyond angry and a few choice words that make the PG-13 list were thrown in my direction that morning. In the end, Jack gave me an ultimatum that if he wasn't allowed to use his own equipment then he would quit and not allow us to use his gear. It was at that moment that I began to realize our team was being held hostage by Jack.

I realized that morning that I had been allowing a slew of negative behaviors because I was operating under the mindset of not upsetting the norm with Jack because I was subconsciously afraid of losing what Jack did for the team. I honestly didn't realize how toxic his attitude had been amongst the group and how bad his lack of commitment and punctuality were impacting the way others in the team viewed my leadership. I was allowing Jack to manipulate me for his benefit and in the end, he gave me an ultimatum that in the moment I wasn't prepared for. His lack of attendance, lack of punctuality, and manipulation of what he could bring to the table were his ways of getting what he wanted from the group and making sure no one called him on it. And for a while he was right. It dawned on me that I was terrified that if he left with his gear and his skills that our worship services would collapse, and I would be immediately let go from my job because of my poor performance leading the group.

That morning that Jack blew up at me we made adjustments in our gear setup so that Jack could use his stuff, which left most of the rest of my team not being able to hear anything except our insanely loud drummer. Our service almost pretty much collapsed anyway. And not because of the audio issues but because the mood on the team was so terrible. Everyone knew what had happened and everything was incredibly awkward because of the tension. The un-Christian hearts and feelings we all had were totally unacceptable and certainly not appropriate for worship leaders on a Sunday. It was the worst Sunday of my life. I felt small, out of control, angry, and really embarrassed that I had somehow let this situation get to this point, and so very publicly.

After that Sunday I spent several days praying to God for answers on how to handle fixing the situation. I also discussed the situation with my lead pastor and apologized for letting the situation become so dramatic and letting it affect worship the way it did. I fully expected to be reprimanded. Instead, my pastor, with a dump truck full of grace, simply said "You probably need to let him go, we can buy some equipment and God will bring us another guitarist in His time." Once again, I was speechless.

"Let him go." I had to wrestle with those words a couple more days. This was church after all; can I really kick someone out? I was appalled by the thought. But how else to deal with someone who had become very destructive to the team. And that's what struck me finally. His behavior had ruined not only my day but others on the team as well that had no stake in the matter and Jack almost pulverized a day of church for the entire congregation through his actions. I realized that I couldn't allow someone to hold my team hostage through his erratic behavior, public disrespect and disunity, and self-serving attitude. It wasn't the fact he wanted to use his gear; I wasn't trying to steal his stuff by any means. It was that I realized he thought he could dictate how decisions were made because he thought he was irreplaceable. His actions demonstrated to me he was there for his own agenda and not for advancing the church's mission or our team goals. He wanted to shine and call the shots and would crush anyone who didn't support that aim. I decided to take Jack up on his offer not to come back. I ran the decision past my lead pastor, and he gave me his support and then I called Jack. I told him that I had made some incorrect assumptions regarding his gear and was sorry. But I also told him that our team would not be operating based on anyone's ultimatums and that if he couldn't be committed to the team and not be able to give to the team joyfully, including his gear, then he would need to step down from the team. I let him know he had handled the situation poorly by making such a public spectacle and not coming to me personally and privately. I also let him know how disappointed I was that his issue with me affected everyone on the team and affected our worship service. Needless to say, he didn't like what I had to say and so he chose not to return to the worship team and, after another few months, the church as well.

It really hurt to lose Jack…for about a week. And then the ministry carried on. We bought some equipment and worked that issue out. More guitarists eventually came our way, some better, some worse, but our team grew and filled the void. Most importantly our team was so much better without the toxic element in our midst, one that we didn't even realize was affecting us so much. It wasn't easy but God provided a way for us to be more healthy, effective, and God-honoring because we were no longer making decisions based on not upsetting someone. We were making choices that brought glory to God, encouragement to our church, and growth to our team.

Through this experience I learned that we as worship leaders cannot allow talent or resources to dictate the directions of our teams. You as a worship leader should be vigilant for these kinds of situations and they will come; I've had more than one Jack in my ministry teams. When people have the talent, resources, or time and buy in to the lie that they are irreplaceable, they can potentially try to leverage what they bring to your team to get their own way. Let me tell you brothers and sisters, no one is irreplaceable in God's Kingdom. God sacrificed His own son for the sake of the church; are you willing to say you are more important than Jesus? We truthfully wouldn't want a church that is based on irreplaceable people. If it were, the church would surely crumble. One of the greatest ways to infect your team is to allow anyone to carry on believing they are irreplaceable and can manipulate you. You need to make decisions based on God's prompting, and not on stroking someone's ego. When you lead and grow your worship team be sure it is not hitched to any one person's abilities or what they can bring to the table because you may find yourself in a hostage negotiation and you never want to negotiate with hostage takers. It will likely get ugly, and it will bring your team down and reduce mission effectiveness. Depend on God's guidance and provision and not on man and you won't be slave to man's ego or nefarious agendas.

Do More Than Just Make Music

If your ministry is structured like mine, then your musicians onboard into the ministry via some sort of audition process. It is my strategy to tell prospect volunteers even at this point that our ministry "does more than just make music". My first point is to tell them that worship ministry carries with it the expectation that we are to serve above and beyond the norm and live our lives as leaders within and outside the church. The other point I convey is that our ministry team spends a lot of time together doing a whole lot more than just rehearsals.

I am an avid believer in the concept of team ministry. Those of us in vocational ministry must have a working sense that we are not on staff to do everything, but rather to equip and mobilize the saints in our congregations for ministry. In the real world this means involving your team members in as many facets of ministry as possible.

Now I could speak to the fact that it's not healthy for you as a leader to try to do everything your ministry requires. Many an egotistical worship leader has tried, and failed, because ego alone is not enough to carry the weight of a multi-pronged ministry like worship arts ministry. But really my point goes beyond that. You can't help but throttle your own ministry. There isn't enough of "you" to fully unleash the Kingdom of God into the world. You have limits. Limits of time, creativity, attention, capacity. If you are the only one planning worship, your services will only ever be as creative or excellent as you can be. If you are the only one engaging in pastoral care responsibilities, your people will feel neglected because there is only so much of you to go around. If you are the only one out there researching new music, or keeping up with technology trends, then you are the lid, the limit, the gate holding back the potential of your ministry. You must find systematic and intentional means to involve your team members in all your processes and systems. Worship plan together. Stage design together. Debrief and evaluate services together. Dream of future team expansion and expression together. I encourage you to refuse to be the reason the Spirit is restrained because you insist on holding ministry tasks too tightly. Our team does all these ministry responsibilities together. Some of them don't even include my presence, regularly. For example, song selections are done as a group in our Green Room during one of our services on Sundays during a service we're not listening to Pastor's message. (We have multiple services). Sometimes weeks are delegating to an individual team member to plan and try their hand a planning a service. As you read in the chapter on our audition process, we include team members at almost every step in the process. I'll discuss more about ways to include team members in the worship planning process in a future chapter. The greater point is healthy teams have members with skin in the game. Few teams have ever thrived with one person at the top dictating every facet of the organization. You absolutely must elevate the value of your team members. This allows your team to flourish by having a constant infusion of creativity, administration, and energy because these things are not all coming from you. The culmination of all this team participation is a ministry that is full, vibrate, wildly creative, excellent in execution, and inclusive. When your people know there is a place for them to express their talents, thoughts, and feelings they will feel ownership and pride in their ministry team and be more deeply invested and committed to its success.

Now this requires you as leader to hold on to the reigns loosely. You have to sacrifice your ego, talent, and position as the most talented, or even simply the one getting paid. You won't be the end all, be all for your ministry. But the more comfortable you get with this reality the greater heights your ministry will soar, and the greater glory God will receive because the ministry you oversee is unleashed to do God-sized things, without being quelched by one person's limitations or insecurities.

Doing more than making music means something else, too. Don't underestimate the importance of just plain old fun together. Team friendships and family culture can be organic and not need an ounce of your focus, but it has been my experience the larger your team grows, the more you should give attention to large, full ministry opportunities to hang out, do ministry together, and love one another in Christ. My worship arts team rotates volunteers each week and so therefore our whole team seldom sees each other all together. I make sure to plan a few events each year where I call the entire team together for just being together, usually over food and some sort of activity. Christmas time is an obvious excuse for this, but we also usually have pre-semester launch events to focus our team for the next season. The last several years we have held Christmas Murder Mystery Dinners. Food, fun, costumes, prizes, the works. It's great fun and we do nothing but just celebrate Christmas and the success of the ministry.

Through the years we've expressed this aspect of serving together in all sorts of ways. It's been poolside BBQs, Fantasy Football leagues, or visiting other churches to worship and see what we can learn or do better. Other times it's as simple as just hosting a hangout at our home. These have been great times of fun, and some of our favorite collective team memories are made at these events. These opportunities can be complex and require a ton of work or it can be really simple. Fun is obviously the goal of these events, but there is a more significant reason for making sure this aspect of your ministry happens regularly. If you don't know it already, worship ministry can get tense. In the midst of rehearsals, sound checks, or services that are complicated or aren't going well there can be mountains of tension among those that participate in worship ministry. It is the deep friendships and familial ties that allow honest conversations and critiques while pursuing excellence that don't result in trampled feelings. When we know, trust, and deeply love each other there are greater levels of trust and compassion. You'll be amazed how much less drama will take place in the tense moments of preparation when the bonds are tight and secure among God's people working together for a common purpose. These ties can happen naturally, but the mark of true leadership is intentionality in influence upon the culture of the team a leader is responsible for serving. I encourage you to craft opportunities for fellowship outside of the regular rhythm of your ministry where your team members can exercise brotherly love and make great relationships.

Team building requires a great deal of intentional work and focus. And to be perfectly blunt, high ropes courses are on the right track, but we can't visit those as often as we need to really be team building. High ropes courses are a team building exercise, not team building culture. A single day spent doing the same activity together as a team simply doesn't produce the results of a healthy and effective ministry team. You must be very intentional about who is on your team, their investment in the culture, and their buy in to the team's vision and fellow team members.

9 – Running a Rehearsal That Flourishes

*Good planning and hard work lead to prosperity,
but hasty shortcuts lead to poverty.*

Proverbs 21:5 NLT

One of the things you'll be doing almost as much as leading a worship service is running a rehearsal. To be honest this is probably the most important time of your week from a work standpoint. Obviously worship services hold the most eternal significance as a part of your ministry but do not make the mistake of undervaluing the precious time of rehearsal. How you spend this time can make or break your worship services and the long-term health of your team. Remember, this is likely the biggest chunk of "face time" you will get with your team members, so it is vitally important that this gathering be intentional and well managed.

It All Starts with YOUR Preparation

Whether your team is small with only a couple people, or large with full choirs or orchestras or some mix in between, there are a lot of moving parts at a rehearsal. You may even be tasked with overseeing a production and A/V team which only further adds pieces to the jigsaw puzzle that is being fully prepped for a coming worship service. I cannot stress enough that when the hour strikes for rehearsal to begin, ***you must always be the most prepared person in the room.*** While it may not be fully in your job description depending on your particular church setting, ***running*** a rehearsal means you are the connective tissue that holds a worship team together. You need to be prepared to answer questions about bass lines or drums parts. You need to be prepared to guide vocalists as to their parts or entrances and exits musically and maybe physically moving on or off the platform. You may need to help troubleshoot a piece of equipment that is not working properly. Sounds overwhelming, doesn't it? Don't stress. I'm not saying you need to be a know-it-all. That's a hopeless goal. But it does mean you should know your content and your gear backwards and forwards. And this includes other people's parts, responsibilities, and *how* (church preferences) your team should be using your church's gear or A/V equipment. This means lots of homework for you. You must show up already knowing your worship plan and your part in it. Mistakes like not knowing your music or not having thought through lighting cues until you show up to practice means you'll be focused on yourself instead of serving your team. And that's my point here. Your job at rehearsal is to be available to lead others and you simply can't do that if you're unprepared. And the bigger your team gets the better your institutional systems have to be to ensure you are prepared. You should have a vision of your rehearsal flow from start to finish and assist your entire team to reach this vision.

If your team is anything like mine it is largely comprised of volunteers. This of course means you're not working with professional musicians or production team members. There will be a lot of questions and at times a lot of handholding. There will also be times where you just don't have an answer prepared and that's ok, too. The idea is that you are prepared enough to be available to help guide others to the answers or help their need to the best of your availability.

Preparation isn't totally up to you either. If you really want your team to shine and to alleviate a ton of headaches for you and your worship team, preparation for the entire team begins long before anyone shows up to a rehearsal.

Making Sure the Team Is Prepared BEFORE Rehearsal

Homework, homework, homework. With my teams, this is a matter of our culture. It's built into our Covenant. It's the expectation when people show up. It's addressed when an individual clearly isn't doing their homework. There is a hard line with our worship team(s) and it is this mantra; Rehearsal is for putting the pieces together and putting the polish on for weekend services, *not for learning music.* It is absolutely vital that you insist your volunteers show up prepared. Now, everyone gets busy and sometimes people show up and they don't have time for homework. There's always room for grace. What you want to be on the lookout for is habits. Is the same person always making excuses? Eventually you need to step in and address the issue. It will make your team achieve a higher excellence standard. Even more than that, it's only fair to the rest of your team that did carve out time to practice or prep materials that the whole team be putting in the same effort.

But let's get real about a facet of having your team prepared for rehearsal. If your team doesn't have good resources, or worse still, *NO* resources from which to practice, you really are shooting yourself in the foot. They are only going to be minimally prepared if you are not setting them up for success. A huge part of this endeavor is ensuring your entire team is operating on the same baseline for how you intend the music you've chosen to be executed. I am borderline psychotic when it comes to our worship team resources. By resources I mean audio files, chord charts, click tracks, vocal rehearsal tracks, music score, lead sheets, lyrics sheet (especially for production). One of the most destructive elements to rehearsals is not providing your team with timely, accurate, reliable, and easily accessible resources. Let me say this as clear as I possibly can...YOUR RESOURCES MUST BE 100% RIGHT! Everything from song arrangement to key signatures to chords must be accurate. Song flow matters, too. It's not good enough to give your team a chart that has one of each section just thrown on a page. Give them the whole song, in the proper order. Your production team will thank you as well so that they can put lyrics on screen in the correct order. I cannot stress this enough. If you want your rehearsals to become exceedingly effective and time efficient, get your people stellar resources to work with and make them available as early as possible so your team can be practicing with them. I've witnessed way too many worship teams utterly frustrated by the time rehearsal is over due largely to songs in wrong keys, wrong chords, or charts that don't match a given audio file. Especially in this day and age, when many Christian artists will all record a version of the same song, you must be very clear which version you're using and make sure your resources match *that* version specifically. This requires you to prepare your resources personally and to go through everything with a fine-toothed comb. This also requires a good bit of musical knowledge sometimes because it may mean writing your own charts and not just pulling something off the internet. If you don't possess these skills find and take a course online or at local education center or scour YouTube on this topic. You may even consider bringing someone in from your team to help with this process who does have the music theory knowledge to help. Thankfully, in this day and age, there are online companies that have gotten really good at providing these resources, but I find them to still only be accurate about 75-80% of the time. Even using these resources, you can't assume what you're purchasing is fully prepped for your team. If you use one of these services, I encourage you to go with one that allows you to edit resources like chord charts before disseminating them to your team.

The reality is when your whole team is working from the same baseline of reliable resources, you'll waste so much less time in rehearsal because there is no guesswork for your team members. This doesn't mean there isn't room for flexibility and creativity, we rearrange songs all the time, but when everyone knows the base music it's easy to then jump off from that point and direct your team on what to add or subtract.

As far as getting the resources to your team, get it out early! We'll talk about a strategy for building your church's song catalog in a coming chapter, but my advice is as soon as you circle around a song that your team will be using, get it prepped ASAP and add it to the pool of resources for your team to practice (we use Planning Center's "Services" for all worship planning and managing our resources). Once you've equipped your team properly, rehearsals become about putting all the moving pieces together for service. You should discover you have more time to talk about more nuanced topics like dynamics, interpretation, syncopation, and more that can sometimes be neglected when you're just trying to figure out what chords everyone needs to play. You should also find that in addition to improved music quality you can focus on other things like worship leader skills and things like heart condition and platform presence. But you have to do the work of prepping great resources to help your team shine.

The need for great resources means you have to carve out intentional time in your work week. You probably need to devote a specific time each week to just resource preparation. In my setting, my team spends most of our Monday mornings focused on resource and A/V prep both for the current coming Sunday and for weeks and months to come. By having this intentional time that starts our week we are able to consistently have resources ready when we need them, and this crucial task doesn't get buried in all the other things that can crop up as the week progresses. There's little chance of resource prep getting shelved because we get it out of the way first whenever we can. Your schedule is going to dictate what works best but be intentional and stick to your specific time.

Now that we've talked about getting your people prepared to come to rehearsal, let's talk about an effective rehearsal schedule once they're there.

Rehearsal A - Z

I don't believe there is one *right* way to run a rehearsal. There are hundreds of things you could do with your time. How you break up your rehearsal flow can vary in a host of different ways and your flow is truly a matter of choice. Through the years, however, I've developed a schedule for rehearsal that I feel makes the most of a few short hours and yet is highly effective at producing results for spiritual growth and technical excellence. I'd like to give my rundown of our rehearsal schedule in the hopes it will give you some ideas to make yours better. I've been using some variation of this schedule for almost a decade now, and a simplified version before that for another five years. This schedule comes from years of fine tuning from personal experience, polling our team members, and picking the brains of other worship pastors/leaders. Like I said, there's no right way, but our schedule works and if you haven't been intentional about your rehearsal schedule before now, I'm praying this will make you evaluate and improve the time you spend leading rehearsals.

Pre-Rehearsal

If you feed them, they will come!....EARLY!

We offer food before rehearsal. Everybody serving on the team signs up for a week's rehearsal and it's their job to bring food for the rest of the team for that week. Depending on the number of people serving on your team, it's a minimal number of times someone has to bring something and the rest of the year they are blessed by being able to just show up to food. At our church our numbers are such that someone really only has to end up bringing a meal to share once a school semester. Dinner doesn't have to be fancy or even home-cooked, it just has to be edible. For real, we've done cereal nights. Yes, someone brought six or seven different types of cereal and milk. It was glorious and the whole team still remembers it.

Why? Why go through the hassle of managing a sign up like that? Time. Time is always against you at rehearsal. Our dinner is supposed to be ready at least 15 minutes before the start of our rehearsal. We kick off rehearsal at 6:00PM so for our purposes, dinner is waiting at 5:45PM. See, in our area we have tons of families with young kids, and we've found starting anything later than 6 causes us to lose participation because it's simply too late for families with kids. Many of our people come straight from work and too many of them were getting stuck in terribly run fast food drive-through lines, trying to get a bite to eat before rehearsal. So, we took the conflict away. By having food ready before rehearsal, people can come, grab some grub, and be in place and wait to start rehearsal on time. And that's the *why*. Having food early means people will be ready to start rehearsal and the battle to make the most of your time begins on time or sometimes even ahead of schedule.

Also, having your space open early ensures people can also come a bit early and load in gear, get a jump on prepping A/V, or just get some socializing in. Giving your people a window of time to come in and be under no pressure to jump in to anything means they can catch up with friends and not waste precious work time later. I also find people will go ahead and ask me questions they had from the homework time. This ability to provide clarity means they feel more prepared to practice and work once we actually get to it during rehearsal. It also gives you some time as their leader to be able to just focus on your team, their lives, and needs. Don't forget about opportunities like this to build relationships with people you're going to be asking so much of.

As a side note, I make it a point to make sure during this time that I'm not doing anything "work" related. I make sure to wrap up everything I'm doing for the church or ministry before 5:45PM and people start arriving. This is for two reasons. The first is to be present for my team. It is important to myself and to them that I greet them warmly when they arrive so that they feel their presence is valued. The other reason is it's a chance to get my head right and de-stress from whatever my day has looked like so that I can be as prepared as I can be to serve my team and give them my all. I encourage you to take this time to "flush" and make sure you are in a great headspace for being with your team. Don't carry your stress or frustration or anything else negative with you once rehearsal dinner hits. Your team will follow your lead with whatever you bring to rehearsal.

This Is Your Time for Discipleship

Rehearsal is your time with your team family. Don't waste it! Let's be real, weekend service is go time! You honestly won't likely get a lot of ministry time with your worship team volunteers on Sundays (or whenever your church worships). As your ministry grows this will become more and more of a reality the more people and moving parts are involved with your services. Your pastor, congregation, and technical problems can and will, very easily, consume your time. If you are concerned about the spiritual growth and health of your team (which you should be), rehearsal is the time to help them be better Christ followers.

At our rehearsals our discipleship time is called LAUNCH, because it launches us into the rest of rehearsal. Friend, in this century, there is no shortage of content and I've largely found that as long as your discipleship content fosters conversation, the format doesn't matter. We've done everything from team member prepared devotions, to video studies, to book studies, and everything in between. Focus on Jesus and becoming more like him and you'll be winning. Find something that focuses on worship theology and/or worship leader development and you're golden. Our Launch time runs roughly 30 minutes and includes about a five-minute study, 10-15 minutes of discussion, and 10-15 minutes of prayer time. We ask for prayer requests and any team member can talk about their life and their needs. Guide this time as best you can to keep it timely, but keep in mind that this time may be some of your volunteers' small group in all reality. Keep some flexibility at heart because sometimes this discipleship time can get deep, and prayer requests may be numerous, and the prayer of righteous people "has great power and produces wonderful results" (James

5:16 NLT). We shoot for 30 minutes but I'd be lying if I didn't tell you LAUNCH has extended for an hour at times over the years. And while it may put a pinch on the rest of rehearsal, I wouldn't trade these times for anything to be a part of my team growing and wrestling with the matters of God and be the best followers of Christ we can be. On the other hand, some nights LAUNCH is quick because people just aren't very chatty, and we're done in less than 20 minutes.

The reality is though if you want Christ centered worship leaders and production team volunteers, it's your job to make sure your rehearsals are pointing the worship team to Jesus, and not just practice for a performance. If you want authentic worshippers leading your church body, then be the champion of building disciples.

I'm also a firm believer that discipleship time at rehearsal is best done at the beginning. While there is an argument to be made about putting God first, and I wholeheartedly agree, the reason I suggest conducting discipleship focus first it is bit more practical. Doing it after you've practiced means your people are spent from the energy usage of working/playing during rehearsal, spent emotionally from going to deep places in worship, and if you're like us and rehearsal is mid-week in the evening, it's been a long day and people are ready to go home. I believe you just don't get the mental focus for discipleship by waiting until the end of rehearsal.

Break It Up

Once we've said "Amen" at the end of our prayer time as a total team, rehearsal gets broken up into several groups for the next thirty minutes or so. We break up into three groups:

+ Vocalists
+ Band
+ Production Team

The Vocalists break out and have a time of just vocal rehearsal. During this time, we sing through most of the songs of our worship set going over hot spot places of importance, communicating vocal cues for entrances and exits, and working out parts and making sure harmonies are tight. This time for vocalists is crucial as once we're on the platform with all the amplified sound, it becomes incredibly difficult to isolate problems and clean things up vocally. This is also a great time to provide more individualized vocal technique coaching. My setting is a fully contemporary worship service style, but we do run a worship choir that includes about a dozen singers in addition to our featured vocalists and our musicians who provide backing vocals as well. The more voices you have the more important a vocals only rehearsal becomes but even a small team of only three singers benefit from the time to make sure they are singing together and not clashing with one another.

Thirty minutes isn't a ton of time, so you'll need to be prepared ahead of time with all your notes of what you feel is important to work on. It helps if you can provide these cues ahead of time (Planning Center's Music Stand app is an amazing tool for sharing notes on chord charts and it's what we use).

Another pro tip, we use our backing track with just the piano track isolated during this time to practice with. Singers typically prefer figuring out parts and notes from piano and it makes it so that any of your vocalists can lead this vocal rehearsal time and no one *needs* to know how to play a piano. A live pianist would be even better but using the track is a great tool to make your vocal time more effective. We include the click track and verbal cues as well because it begins the process of training new vocalists to get used to performing with click track.

While we're on the topic of vocalists I want to share with you our Vocalist Development Process. We've instituted a tiered system when it comes to vocalists in recent years, and I have to say the system we have developed I wish was something I had in place years ago as it would have saved me, and numbers of volunteers, a lot of frustration. We have three tiers, and every vocalist has to progress through the system in order to be eligible to be a lead singer. Tier I is where everyone starts with our team as a member of our Worship Choir. Tier II are backing vocalists and Tier III are lead-capable, worship leaders. Talent certainly helps but it is a system that values serving others on the team as well as demonstrated vocal and worship leading skills, and time devoted to serving the ministry and the church. Built into the DNA of the system is also intentionality on vocal technique development. In the Resource section at the end of this book I've published our Vocalist Tier System and actual benchmarks and responsibilities of each Vocalist Tier. The important thing I want to communicate is that on our team it is very clear what singers' expectations are and how to progress to roles of greater leadership responsibility. It's not a matter of showing up and being the most talented singer, we prioritize servant leadership more and the Tier system fosters and protects that. Each Tier above Tier I has its own audition process team members take part in, just like our initial audition process.

Our vocal rehearsal time includes all tiers of singers and is a crucial time to help our singers develop and grow, especially those interested in moving up the tier system. This way newer, less experienced singers are immersed in our expectations and coaching right alongside our veterans.

The second group we break into is the Platform Band. During this time our instrumentalists head to the platform and have thirty minutes to setup their gear and instruments, get their in-ear monitors roughly mixed, maybe have a few minutes to start practicing some music, and be in place for the Production Team to make sure they are in the proper positions for lighting or video.

The third group, the Production Team, has the same thirty minutes to prep A/V as much as they can. This is their time to prep mics, type lyrics, set lighting cues, tidy the platform, or train on new equipment or best practices for our tech systems. Now I promise, your Production Team will always wish for more time here, but this time is so valuable for them to be able to prep without having the full team on the platform making demands of them for sound adjustments or lyrics cues, etc. To be frank, we prep a lot of A/V elements before rehearsal at our church and the Production Team is still usually crunched for time in these thirty minutes of prep. This is also really important time that can be spent training new volunteers while the full rehearsal hasn't gotten under way just yet. The aim, however, is for the Production Team to be ready to begin running service elements as a part of the rehearsal by the time the 30 minutes is up. That way the Production Volunteers are focused on *running* cues with the whole team, and not prepping cues.

Back Together Again

If you've been doing the math in your head you should hopefully know at this point we've hit about 7:00PM at rehearsal; thirty minutes for LAUNCH, thirty minutes for breakout groups. Now is the time for *ALL* that preparation to pay off. At this point we pull the whole team together and everyone should be ready to start putting the pieces together and putting the polish on for service. It's time for full sound, full lights, get those motion backgrounds going, make sure that the hazer is belching out that beautiful atmosphere! Now is the time for "practice like you play". If you intend to do something Sunday, you better be doing it now! You should progress through each service element one by one, in order, to make sure it's ready. You're checking videos, and backing tracks, camera angles, and lighting transitions. If it's your role to oversee something for your church during service, go over it during rehearsal.

As far as practicing music, here are some recommendations for running through songs. Give your notes to the band first before you run though anything. Make sure you're communicating things you've added or subtracted from the base song. Don't make them guess, let them know how you want the song to flow and insist they make notes. Even if your musicians memorize their music (lucky you!), having them write down notes in some way helps it to stick so they don't forget and blow it.

Run every song twice, no matter what. Practice makes perfect and you'll hear things the second time through, good and bad things you didn't hear the first time. Trust me, even if you think your team nailed a song the first pass through, I promise you that someone on your team isn't confident about something and needs the additional run through. If you notice something isn't right, fix it! Don't hope it will go away. Hammer a section until it is right and then run the WHOLE song again. After the second run through ask if anyone has any questions, including your Production Team, address issues or concerns, and if needed for polish or clarity, run the song again. That's at least 3 run throughs. Unless the song is a golden oldie for your team your team needs this many to feel confident in the craft. Again, let me stress including your Production Team through this whole process. Make sure they are good to go as well before moving forward to the next service element or song. Keep in mind they need to practice their cues also to be ready for Sunday!

All the while, keep in mind that if you're working with volunteers, you should be building your team up and building confidence. Make sure to compliment moments or songs that go well and people who are doing a great job or fixing mistakes. Celebrate improvement and be specific. On the regular I have our team play a game I call "Who Were You Listening To, and What Did They Do?" It's an intentional way to make sure our team is listening to each other and playing together but also celebrating each other's accomplishments. I'll call on a team member and ask them "Who were you listening to, and what did they do?" and that person will name someone and talk about something specific like "That bass line rocked" or "Your vocals were really on pitch" or even "I think your drum fill was just a bit behind the click" and then we can work on it. The important thing is that when you do fix something, cheer it on. When your folks leave, they should feel Sunday will be a piece of cake, not something to dread the rest of the week because they're nervous.

Wrapping Up

Our Rehearsal runs two and a half hours which means we are scheduled to wrap up by 8:30PM. Very seldom do I ever run over. I value people's precious time and you should, too. If you've done the appropriate prep work, people do their homework, and you've led an effective and efficient rehearsal, then you should have no problem ending on time or early.

The reality is you likely will need to always end five to ten minutes early for a couple reasons. If you are running our Audition Process, you will likely have some conversations and evaluations to conduct with the team regarding people in the process. It is also vitally important that you make yourself available to your team at the end of the night. I learned about myself some years ago that for whatever reason I come across as intimidating. As much as I hate the impression, there is something about my demeanor that makes people naturally afraid to approach me with personal issues or questions. To combat this, I've become very intentional about announcing at the end of rehearsal that I'm available if anyone needs anything and if they need to talk, I'd love to hear from them. Most weeks nothing happens but every so often someone comes to talk. Sometimes it is technical, more often times it's something spiritual or personal. End your rehearsal a few minutes early and just be prepared to be a set of listening ears. When we practice, we're worshipping, and the Holy Spirit is still ministering to your volunteers even in the midst of rehearsal and you can be there to help guide and to pray for your worship family as needs arise.

Have Fun!

Rehearsals are busy. Rehearsals are complicated. Rehearsals are noisy. Rehearsal is controlled chaos. Sometimes I feel like I'm on a ride and my grip is just barely clinging on, keeping me seated. And rehcarsals can get sideways in a hurry. One song can turn into a giant struggle bus and suddenly it seems the whole rehearsal crashes and burns. One piece of equipment can fail and derail the whole affair. The important thing to always remember is that it is a privilege to be a part of God's kingdom work in the special expression of the worship arts. The first two fruits of the Spirit are love and joy. If we are to be lead worshippers, then our time together should be marked by radical joy that only the Holy Spirit can bring out in our lives.

There are many opportunities in our rehearsal time for natural frustrations to creep in. We don't have to manufacture challenges; they will come our way. That's why it's important for those of us who run rehearsals to make sure we are cultivating joy and blessings by being a part of the worship ministries we oversee. It boils down to this; please make sure you are having fun serving together. You will spend a ton of time together and if you're not having fun together it will become tedious. Your people will burn out, dread participating, and quit on you. Allow time for jokes and stories and goofing off. Laugh with each other when songs crash and burn. Celebrate the moments when God moves and worship is just **jam up amazing** and you can't wait for your whole church to experience what God has already done in rehearsal! Don't be so focused on the nuance of *stuff* that you neglect the nuance of *ministry* or *community*. After all, we're trying to build lifestyle worship, and life happens way more between the songs than during.

Rehearsal Schedule

> ➢ 5:45 – 6:05 – Dinner / Worship Auditorium Open
> ➢ 6:00 – 6:30 – LAUNCH
> ➢ 6:30 – 7:00 – Vocal Rehearsal / Band Setup / Production Prep

- ➤ 7:00 – 8:20 – Full Run Through Rehearsal
- ➤ 8:20 – 8:30 – Audition Evaluations / Final Details / Ministry Time
- ➤ 5:45 – 8:30 – Fun

10 – Building and Maintaining Your Church's Song Catalog

He has given me a new song to sing,
a hymn of praise to our God.
Many will see what he has done and be amazed.
They will put their trust in the Lord.

Psalm: 40:3 NLT

I'm going to accuse you of something. I'm really confident you're probably doing it. And you should seriously stop doing it. Or at least maybe don't do it nearly as often as you are right now. You won't go to jail for it, but it's really pretty terrible and you really need to change your ways.

OK…here's the accusation…

You're using music *YOU* like to lead worship!

You're a terrible human being.

Alright, I'm kidding…kind of.

If you're truly honest with yourself then you'll probably recognize that you're choosing music as the worship leader for your church that is biased by your tastes and preferences in music.

Quite honestly, there's nothing morally wrong with this. The reality is someone has to choose music for your church to utilize for worship. But if you're like I *used* to be, and if you're like WAY too many worship leaders out there, you're choosing music all by yourself. I can't insist enough how much this is a facet of your worship ministry that you should put a stop to as soon as possible. Let's discuss why.

Many People, One Church

If you've spent time in God's church at all, you know that the church is made of a bunch of people. And the people that we lead in worship are different. Different from you. They are not a gathering of clones of the same person. Each person that sits in the seats in your church has a different story, a different upbringing, different experiences, unique traumas, and individual accomplishments all of which shape their own unique perspective of life, church, family, work, and priorities. This is the beautiful thing about what God has done through our Lord, Jesus. He has brought many people, from many backgrounds and cultures into His family (Romans 8). This family is His church. This means each time your church gets together it is not homogenous. It's a terrible mistake to assume that every soul attending a worship service is anywhere close to being similar to the person sitting right next to them. Even within a nuclear family, everyone is going to be different. God's church is made of many parts of one body, but that body is diverse with each part bringing something unique to function of the whole (1 Corinthains 12:12-27)

Imagine, just for a minute, you put one hundred of your closest friends in a room together for dinner. It's your job to feed everyone in the room and you decide everyone is going to eat a sandwich because you love sandwiches. You've already disappointed a few people because they think sandwiches aren't for dinner. Then you decide you're going to put salami on those sandwiches for everyone because salami is your favorite. You just lost some more people who can't stand salami. To finish it all off, you've decided that since you absolutely love anchovies, that's how you're going to dress the sandwiches. You just lost almost everybody else in the room who can't stand anchovies. And then the worst thing you do is make that room full of your friends eat the same salami and anchovy sandwich four or five times in a row. Now, your one weird friend (you know who I'm talking about) is probably happy because they are going to like anything you like because they are *that* friend, but everyone else leaves the evening questioning your judgment and runs out to Five Guys to grab something they'll actually eat.

In a sense, this is what many worship leaders do to their congregations. A single individual makes worship choices based on stylistic choices. In all honesty, we can't help it, we like what we like. You are inherently biased and you're probably going to make creative choices based on your own preferences. It is what we do, we tend to operate in our comfort zones. We might go out a limb from time to time, but left to our devices, our music selection is going to be heavily influenced by what we feel is "good music" or even "what's popular" with other churches.

I want to strongly encourage you to stop selecting worship and particularly music content in this manner. You simply must get out of your own bubble when it comes to planning your services. Do you really want to feed your friends a salami and anchovy sandwich for four or five songs in a row? If you love your local church, I sincerely doubt that's the menu you want to bring to Sunday morning. Let me encourage you to elevate your leadership to a more collaboartive level and start gathering other members of your team and church to be led by the Holy Spirit together while planning. Your worship services need to be a reflective cross-section of the diversity of your congregation and if you are making choices in isolation there is absolutely no way your worship services are going to speak to various perspectives that show up to your church.

Now you may be asking, "Why does it matter?" Bluntly, the answer is you should be terrified of being a lid to the Holy Spirit. Realize, if your services are only ever as creative as you can muster on your own, you are going to be the maximum capacity your church will reach. This goes for all creative aspects of your services. Videos, skits, dance, sign language, stage designs, all of these elements will be limited by the amount of creativity in your ministry, and you might be highly creative, but more minds equal more ideas and influences that come to bear and leave their mark on your ministry. It will take good systems and organization for sure, as endless ideas and no action is not a win either; nothing gets done. But start thinking "team ministry", not "my ministry". The Holy Spirit is for all believers to be ministered to and sometimes He needs to say things in ways that probably aren't your jam, or speak to people that have different tastes, heritage, and experiences than you.

There are many ways you can accomplish strategic worship planning involving other individuals from your church. And each type of creative element such as videos or skits will need systems or strategies to involve others for creative planning, but I want to spend the rest of this chapter focusing on music selections (mostly). I feel song choices have the greatest ongoing impact on our services and often influence choices for other elements. Music is often the hardest creative element to get people to collaborate on because music is so personal to people. I feel our system can be adapted for most other creative elements you might plan and therefore can apply broadly across the board. So let me lay out how our ministry builds and utilizes a living, breathing, and adaptable song catalog that represents the cross-section of our people and is highly diverse and not planned in isolation by myself.

You Need Help! Throw a Party!

That right, it's party time!

The first major core piece of our process is the Music Selection Party. But first let's back up and discuss how we get to the party.

Before you can party, you have to be a collector.

We collect music non-stop. Now, notice my very intentional word "collect". Collect does not mean **use**. Collecting songs means compiling an ongoing list of potentials. We are constantly collecting from anywhere and everywhere. The awesome thing about living in the 21st century is there are resources *everywhere*. Online, on the radio, publishing companies, streaming services, backing track websites, church members, fellow church staff, worship team members, and yes, you can still buy physical albums (I know, old school, but it works!). There are literally sources for potentials surrounding you and your ministry all the time. For our ministry, we take requests all the time. They come in from our church members, our staff members, our worship team members, and our family members. There are resources out there such as Song Discovery that all they do is send you new, potential worship music. There are entire conferences where music publishing companies will show up with new content just for people to sit and listen for hours to new offerings for choral music. We also do a ministry survey at some time close to our Music Selection Parties to get feedback from team members to gauge the health of the Worship Ministry, but it is also a forum where we ask for suggestions for songs to use for worship. We also ask our team which songs they are sick of and that they would like to see retired. We'll get to maintaining your ongoing song catalog in a bit. In all of the sources, do your best to get as much information as possible on song versions, albums, streaming service links, etc. That way when you're evaluating songs and prepping music you know which version someone suggested. As you probably know, most Christian and worship songs these days have radio and/or live versions, and multiple artists will often record the same song. Make sure you are tracking the version someone has suggested that the Holy Spirit speaks through. Some versions are just flat out better musically or more suited to congregational worship.

We collect. Non-stop.

This is not the place to weed *anything* out. Put a song on the list, thank people for their suggestions, and go back to living your life. You'll get to the vetting process soon. For now build your list. Collect, collect, collect!

Over time you should have a crazy amount of music on your list. If you cultivate the culture of collecting well over a long enough arc of time, you should never hurt for potential new music. In fact, the bigger challenge you will face should be weeding down all the music you've collected. At times for me it's been fifty songs on the list! It will depend on how often your ministry has a Music Selection Party and works through your list. And that is something you and your leadership team will need to figure out before you can party; how often to have a Music Selection Party. For my church, we run almost all our ministry activities on a semester-based calendar, very similar to a university calendar. So as a part of this natural cycle in our church we typically have a Music Selection Party during our Fall and Spring Semesters. You will have to discern what is a healthy pattern for your ministry based on your circumstances but once you have that nailed down, calendar the event and then publicize it to who you will be including in the process. At my church we include our entire worship team including the Production Team, our student worship team, and any staff that are interested in being involved as well as any adult or teen aged family members of those groups of people. The Music Selection Party will be your ministry's initial evaluation part of the process of planning worship but there is one more thing to do before you can party with your team.

The one task that is best for only one or two people to do before the Music Selection Party is vet the song list for theological accuracy. This needs to be someone with spiritual authority and hopefully theological and doctrinal education. Don't take bad theology to your team for them to even consider. In my ministry, my wife and I go through our song list and listen to everything and check lyrics to make sure songs are congruent with our church's theological stance and statement of beliefs. When in doubt bring in some other spiritual authority such as your lead pastor, a deacon, or a trusted and spiritually wise member of your worship team. This will be a significant body of work to undertake sometimes, and it may take some time (my wife and I will do this driving on longer trips), but it is your responsibility as overseer of the ministry to ensure this takes place. We usually whittle the list down in this process to around twenty-five to thirty songs. Remember, this is not a place for you to weed out things you don't like because of style. Your whole goal is to bring in diversity of creativity to your services. It's not about you, so allow your team to be a part of those decisions. Once you've flushed anything with inaccurate theology, build your final list, and get ready to party!

The Music Selection Party should be exactly that...a party! The actual goal is to scale down your list of potentials into your list of final selections that you are going to prepare resources and introduce into your song catalog. But the whole exercise is better wrapped in a whole lot of fun and fellowship. I'm talking food, great atmosphere, fun games. Something your people don't want to leave. Don't be afraid of decorations. The truth is it's going to take a while to do a Music Selection Party, so you want your team to have such a great time they don't quite realize how long you're all hanging out. We usually plan for about four hours for our events in order to get through, on average, about twenty-five songs. Make sure to hold it somewhere cozy and fun. We tend to use our backstage Green Room, because it has comfy couches, lamp lighting instead of overhead clinical lighting, and access to snacks and drinks. Be sure to have some great music bumping as people arrive and consider having snacks available and something fun going on as people are waiting to start the event (game, trivia, etc.).

Once you start Music Selection Party, the first thing you're going to want to do is equip your people with the tools for evaluating all the songs they are about to start listening to. This is a time for coaching. Anyone can decide if they like something because of the song style, but there is a lot more that goes into evaluating a song for congregational use than just style. Remember that in all of this you are singing to the Lord, and to YOUR church. Remind your people it is not about them and their preferences, but rather the people that are coming seeking an encounter with the Lord at worship service time. Make sure your team has their church family at heart throughout the entire day together, and how God would speak and minister to them through music and worship. Your church probably has an identity and things you are specifically looking for in music choices, so convey these ideals to your team. Just because an Elevation Worship song is hot, doesn't mean it applies to your church body. There's nothing wrong with exposing your church to something unique and different on occasion, but the greater body of work that is your song catalog should be aimed at meeting your people where they are. Making people uncomfortable just for creativity's sake is not behaving as His church. You will need to spend some time explaining to your team your ideals, what they mean, and what you're specifically looking for, or not looking for, so make sure to build this time in at the beginning of your party. This is the list we use (feel free to borrow or expand any of this):

- Horizontal vs. Vertical vs. Introspective vs. Top-Down Worship
- Radio / Recognizable
- Singable
- Vocal Range
- Energy – Hi, Med, Low
- Joyful / Celebration (Worship should be uplifting)
- Gender Bias / Appeal (We try to keep most of our music appealing to men in the church)
- Corporate vs. Special Music (Some songs aren't meant for congregational use, but we may find a special use for them)
- Special Use (such as Christmas, Easter, Communion, Baptism, Mother's/Father's Day, etc.)
- Can our current team actually play this song and pull it off well?

Now the fun part, listening to and evaluating new tunes for the rest of the day. Any true music lover is going to be stoked for this time. As busy as most of us are these days, a day of just music should be a welcome break from the pace of life. As you are evaluating each song at your Music Selection Party, be sure to provide a list of the music you're listening to and a means for you and your team to make notes. Make sure your people know at the start what your target number of songs is. For our ministry, we strive to narrow down the list to about ten to twelve new songs per semester. This is really the maximum number of new songs we find we're able to introduce and teach to our congregation in a given semester and not overwhelm our people with just new songs all the time. Your songs do take time to plant themselves into the life of your church and you don't want to be constantly using music no one knows. But your ministry may look different so please make sure your final list reflects your church's reality.

After we take a listen, we briefly discuss the song's merits and faults, make some notes and then move on to the next song. Your job is to keep things moving. We don't necessarily play the entire song, just maybe it's highlights. Once you have the general sense of the songs, move to discussion and then move on. If you end up going through as much music as we do, it is vital to keep a healthy pace moving through all the content. Personally, I love voicing contrasting opinions throughout the discussion. It forces people to defend their opinions more than just "I liked it". If someone says something about the lyrics being good, ask them something about the lyrics specifically, or maybe even argue something against the lyrics that might be controversial. The goal is not to be a jerk, but rather to really dissect songs that will have a huge impact on your church family and force your team to either stand for the song(s) or weed them out. You should be convicted to pick the absolute best for your church's worship services so make sure the discussion is meaty and fruitful.

Once we've listened to every song, we'll then go around the room and ask for everyone's top choices, maybe top three, maybe top five. The result should become pretty apparent. Almost every Music Selection Party I've conducted through the years there's usually a really clear list of winners by the time we've finished voting. Since we conduct our Music Selection Party with our youth worship ministry as well, we do allow for a modified list for our youth that might include one or two different songs that are more youth oriented. However, by combining teams, it ensures we are worshipping together across all ministries within our church. This breeds unity among our generational groups and is a really wonderful thing to witness in the life of our church. This also means when our youth worship teams serve with us during our main Sunday services, they already know the content. A unified approach also allows us to be better stewards of church resources because we're able to purchase, prepare, and use the same resources such as song charts and click tracks/backing loops. And I'm sure your lead pastor and your church elders will be thrilled with spending less money!

In the years we've used this process for new music, our church loves the music we worship with because it ends up being a cross-sectional representation of most of our people's tastes and heritages because in a sense, our entire church has had a hand in music selection. We can't make everyone happy all the time, but we definitely make most people happy most of the time, which is no easy feat. We also find as a byproduct of the Music Selection Party process we almost always are using the music found on lists like CCLI's top usage lists, *without* having to keep up with their lists. In fact, most of the time we find ourselves ahead of the curve on most of those songs. This keeps our church relevant and up to date and not stuck in the Christian/Worship scene from five years ago. As well, our Worship Team loves our song catalog because they had a hand in crafting it and its not me dictating to them the music we're going to use. When it is not based on me and my style preferences, our team has way more passion behind what we're working on, and I'm sure that's something you'd love to see on your team. Who wouldn't?

You Need Help…Seriously!

There's more work to be done. The work again includes your team at large. Once again, your team having skin in the game is healthy for your team. This aspect of the process isn't music focused per se, but it could be. There are two other elements we include when we ask our team members for song selections that I want to mention. The first is subjective feedback on our worship ministry. I mentioned earlier in this chapter gauging the health of your ministry as being a part of this process. This is where this comes into action and how we go about doing it. Not only can you glean useful help when it comes to having a well-rounded song catalog, your team will likely have all kinds of opinions and perspectives on the experience of serving on your church's worship ministry. Instead of guessing what they think about whether their time spent serving with the team is worthwhile and a blessing to their walk with Christ, ASK THEM!

During the lead up to our Music Selection Party, our form submission asking for song suggestions will also ask some very specific but open-ended questions. In other words, avoid yes or no questions. Instead ask some of the following questions:

> ➤ Please describe how you have grown spiritually as a result of being a member of WAT?
>
> ➤ If you could run rehearsal differently, what would you choose to do?

> If you were telling someone about the worship team who doesn't go to our church, how would you describe our team?
> What's the one thing that frustrates you about serving with the worship team and how might you make it better?
> What do you look forward to most on weeks you serve with WAT?
> Describe what you feel is the biggest win our ministry has experienced since Easter Sunday (or pick a random date)?

Ask whatever you want! Think through the various tasks or events your team does regularly and ask for them to comment on them, the good and the bad. The goal for you is to compile constructive feedback. You're looking for tangible responses with possibilities for improvement. Some of the most insightful times of my ministry have been when I have gotten feedback directly from my team members. More often than not, a team member would convey some issue with how our ministry runs, with me thinking that particular aspect was really great, when in fact our team was not enjoying it.

There was a season when I had our team working through some video driven content that covered various worship leader topics. I thought the material was great and was teaching our team really strong content that they needed. After some feedback, however, it was brought to my attention that members of our team weren't thrilled with the format of the content because it left little room for discussion amongst the team and felt the materials were a bit thin spiritually. Until then I had no clue and had I not asked I would have continued plowing through, my team hating the experience all the while. A good leader is in tune with his or her team and intentionally provides opportunities for team members to have a voice. Not every thought or idea is good or even valid, obviously, and we as leaders must strive to be discerning when it comes to the opinions of the masses, but often times your team having a voice, feeling heard, and having input on your ministry's processes will do wonders for loyalty and team buy-in.

Remember to lay your ego aside in these times. You want an awesome worship ministry, remember? You are not the only one who sees how things work, or how they can be improved. Be careful to not allow yourself to confuse critique of your ministry's systems as criticism of you personally. Some of my biggest problems have been brought to light and addressed by folks who have been my biggest, loyal supporters and loved me the most. And others who have been some of my biggest detractors and headaches flake out without ever saying a word as to why they didn't jive in our system. When you ask for feedback, and I'm insisting you do for the good of your ministry, be humble enough to accept it and wrestle with the feedback and possible solutions to improve your ministry efforts. It's not about you, remember?

Weed Out The Old

Ok, things are clicking, and you have a song catalog and you're getting great music suggestions all the time and great regular feedback about the state of the universe that is your team. …… And then the rumblings start.

People are sick of the music you're using.

It might start at rehearsal. Someone comments about how many times your team has played a song. Maybe someone is bold enough to blurt out they hate a song you're practicing for this Sunday.

Hate.

And it's your favorite song.

Or worse…your lead pastor tells you that you've overplayed a certain tune and asks for you to quit choosing it.

Or worse yet…. your congregation stops participating when that golden oldie you have been doing for a decade starts, you know…"Mighty To Save".

"But they've always loved that song!"

It happens to the best of us.

It happens to me a lot less now.

That's because maintaining our song catalog is a proactive process. The suggestion form we put out to the team also includes a request for feedback on songs from the current catalog the people don't like. We usually ask for the top five LEAST favorite songs in the catalog. And then we follow up with, of those five, which song will make you vomit if you have to play it one more time.

This part of the process can be brutal so steel your heart. Its painful to see your favorite songs come up as the most voted for despised song. But here's the reality, if your team is done with it and hates it, your church might be, too. Do you really want to force feed your people stale, old, overused, and irrelevant worship music?

There is certainly a balance to maintaining fresh vibrant choices with familiarity. You are a fool to try to use all new music in the course of a single service. But your song catalog should have life to it and not be a walking corpse filled with music from eight years ago. By taking a serious look at your team's feelings on the music you're using, you're ensuring that you're not complacent about what you're utilizing and its impact on your congregation and your church's worship environment.

When we have all the forms submitted, our team tallies up the votes for disliked songs. Once we have a final tally, we'll use our best judgement as to which songs it is time to retire. Let's be real, sometimes our team hates a song but every time we worship with it on Sunday our congregation responds, and the Lord is praised and exalted intensely and so we keep that song. But remember, if you're doing regular Music Selection Parties, you're going to be adding a significant amount of music regularly. You have to weed some music out as you go, or your song catalog will become too bloated, and you'll never use everything anyway. It can be sad to say goodbye to some of our favorite songs, but the payoff is a song catalog that is lean, fresh, and much more in tune to the people of your ministry and congregation.

What Do You Mean You Want Hymns?

For my brothers and sisters serving in predominantly contemporary settings you may have one other aspect of your song catalog that presents a challenge you're facing. The "Worship Wars" are not over.

If you're younger or didn't come up in a more traditional church setting, you may not be familiar with that term. Others of us lived through it, some of us painfully. The "Worship Wars" was period not long ago where established churches experienced a great deal of tension and turmoil over whether or not to abandon the traditional style of worship, largely using time-tested codified hymns in favor of the budding contemporary approach using modern praise and worship style music by contemporary recording artists and churches. Churches tried many different ways to test these waters and decide who they were going to be and at times it got ugly I'm sad to say. Some churches fought the war so much there were actual church splits over the debate. The shifting culture of worship experiences during those times was life changing for some, and heart breaking for others.

These days most churches have settled on their identity as to whether they are traditional or contemporary, but it is my opinion that the "Worship Wars" still continue, even in my current setting that is fully contemporary. I still have church members (and no, they're not all old people) ask me about hymns and requests for us to sing them. The conversations are less and less these days, but I still receive them often enough to know you will too and to offer a solution. I encourage you to be sensitive to the reality that the Church has history, heritage, and tradition. Your church likely has history, heritage, and tradition. Even if you're serving in a brand-new church launch (been there, done that, got the T-shirt) your church leadership likely comes from places of ministry that had these things and therefore will carry over into your new church. I encourage you to honor the history you stand upon that belongs to the Bride of Christ.

The (Imperfect) Solution - The "Revival"

The word "revival" means "a period of renewed religious interest" but it also means "a new presentation or publication of something old"[1]. I love when words have double meanings that both equally apply to a situation. I get the same feeling from an easter egg buried in a movie or video game. Something mysterious and fun.

We use this word to refer to a specific category of music that we work to include in our song catalog. This is usually one

1 "Revival." Merriam-Webster.com Dictionary, Merriam-Webster, https://www.merriam-webster.com/dictionary/revival. Accessed 17 Jan. 2024.

of the hardest categories to cultivate because it has to be handled intentionally and with skill and discernment.

A "Revival" in our song catalog meets one of two criteria. 1. It's an old hymn that has been re-worked and updated stylistically so as to be appropriate for a modern worship team to be able to play or 2. It's a praise and worship song from early in the contemporary worship movement. Either way it is a song that is timeless and has substantial value in order to continue to be used. So, a "revival" might be a reworked version of "The Old Rugged Cross" or somebody's cover of "Open the Eyes of My Heart". Believe it or not "Open the Eyes of My Heart" is over twenty years old.

History. Heritage. Tradition. Treasure.

We do our best to keep a running list of revivals that we can include from time to time in our services. Our goal is somewhere around once a month to include a revival in our worship service. Depending on the season our church is in it might be way more, and it might be way less. But we do our best to flavor our services with a little heritage here and there and honor the saints and their art who came before us. You may need to be extra intentional about seeking out revivals because they don't tend to be on people's favorites lists and these aren't necessarily the songs that get a lot of radio or streaming service play time. But intentionally including these in your song catalog helps ensure a system for music selections that answers most of the calls for hymns. But it's not a perfect solution.

I personally find it to be impossible for our ministry to be all things to all people. Even in my fully contemporary setting I have church members who lean on me really hard for us to sing more hymns. The truth is hymns weren't written for rock bands or atmospheric pad samples. It is honestly really challenging to rearrange a hymn and have it work and be relevant to modern congregations. It's harder still as a worship leader to find those arrangements. And even when you do, the re-working of a treasured hymn may be off-putting to some. You can't and won't make everybody happy. Instead of being all things to all people our ministry has adopted the culture of being "most things to most people". We'll never make everyone happy with the songs we choose whatever era they come from. But by being intentional about including occasional selections that have some history and some age, most of our people have that itch scratched for that "old time gospel" and appreciate that our church honors where we've come from as a body of believers. It's not perfect but having an intentional revival system ensures that our song selections speak to our congregation members whose faith is bolstered by something familiar that was part of their faith journey long ago and reminds them of why they choose to believe in our Lord, Jesus.

Adopting these strategies of intentional collaboration and careful selection should yield positive results. You should have a diverse selection of music in your song catalog to choose from. You should also have a song catalog that is reflective of and responsive to your church's own personality and voice. You should have a music ministry that is cutting edge and one that is on point or ahead of the trends in contemporary music and yet honors time honored and treasured music selections from our church heritage. You will also have a layer insulation as leader against accusations that your worship team only picks the music you like. Considering adding these systems to your ministry to gain these healthy benefits.

11 – Worship Planning Strategies

When people do not accept divine guidance, they run wild.
But whoever obeys the law is joyful.

Proverbs 29:18 NLT

As your church's primary worship leader, whether you're filling a pastoral role or a functional musician role, you'll be heavily involved in planning worship services. You may have a lot of leeway as Worship Pastor or be confined to oversight of your lead pastor or Music Minister but I would venture to say you're going to have a significant amount of influence over the content and structure of your church's worship services. To be the best servant in your role requires that you spend a lot of your time planning for the future and crafting services for upcoming weeks, months, and maybe even years. In all of these duties, let me give you some things to think about that will help provide some structure to the ongoing nature of planning and implementation. These are some aspects of worship ministry that I have learned from others along my journey, learned from experience planning worship services for over 25 years, and learned from working for and with various lead and associate pastors.

The First Step of Planning is PREplanning

If you haven't learned one particular principle yet, you will soon. The principle is that you don't toil in ministry in a vacuum. Each one of us, even in the smallest churches, have people that we work with to advance the cause for Christ. You may be teamed with pastoral staff, or you may be assisted by the lay leadership of your church body, either way you're collaborating with other people. Seeing as how you are reading this book about developing as the person who oversees a worship ministry, I'm going to make the guess that you are probably not the lead pastor of your church. If you are the lead pastor and you're overseeing the worship ministry for your church, bless you! I don't how you're still breathing. Go hire someone to run worship ministry at your church, yesterday! For the rest of us it means you likely are working *for* somebody. This means you report to someone who has a greater responsibility for the organization and greater oversight over its vision, mission, and message being guided by the Holy Spirit. Your planning should take this into account.

If nothing else, you need to know what your lead pastor is going to be teaching on. I've have been in church settings where we had a fully fleshed out message series calendar that stretched out eighteen months into the future. It was glorious. I knew what topics and what scripture was going to be covered and how each series was going to be branded and packaged and marketed to our community. I had months in advance to pray for guidance, brainstorm, plan, and implement content that reinforced the messages we taught. We found ways to incorporate worship with outreach and evangelism. We wove church-wide small group studies into Sunday morning expression. It was a thing of beauty to behold.

I've also served in church settings where the lead pastor himself didn't know what he was teaching until he came up with it the Wednesday or Thursday before Sunday. To be fair, he was bi-vocational and had limited time to devote to the small church at the time. But it made for choppy, disconnected, and incoherent Sunday services.

The lesson learned is that good worship planning first starts with knowing the desired end result. You need to be asking questions of your leadership and discussing these matters in the appropriate meetings or gatherings. What message is the church conveying or what message does your church *hope* to convey? Weekly, monthly, yearly? Who is leading the charge for that message, and can you maximize collaboration with that person or team so that you can plan coherent Sunday services that flow well and don't leave your congregation confused or bored? Are you reinforcing what usually comes after the music, the message, or are you a distraction from it? What else is going on in the life of your church that your ministry can be congruent with?

Now trust me, I get it that it can be really challenging in your circumstance to get the needed information to have those kinds of discussions at your church. Remember the pastor that I mentioned that planned his message a few days before preaching it? It's almost impossible to plan worship that is forward thinking and really dialed in to the life of the church in this kind of setting. I've lived that season and it's really frustrating. However, let me issue you this challenge; you can be the force that helps implement this kind of strategic thinking at your church. You can be the advocate for change and improvement, just be prepared to shoulder most of the work to get it running. Strive to be the voice that insists on future thinking. There are endless books out there about church vision planning and church calendaring so I won't even begin to try to give you those kinds of systems here, but the point is your worship services will flourish when there is a common purpose as a church, or at the least, as a staff. If you're not getting it already, ask your lead pastor for a message plan and tell him its so that you can serve his messages better. Ask the other leaders in your church how your ministry can reinforce what's going on in their neck of the woods. And if you find yourself in a setting where your pastor just plain refuses to collaborate, and they are out there, that makes the song selection process we discussed in a previous chapter all that more important. At least in that kind of situation your music is more closely speaking to your church's felt needs and that aids in helping your worship services convey clear, important messages to your congregation. We'll talk in a moment about how on the nose you need to be in worship about your church's message, but each service should have a defined focus that helps those that attend take a step closer to Jesus or a step closer to accomplishing the church's vision and mission.

The idea is to start with the end in mind. Then allow the Holy Spirit to guide you to craft a road map that will take your church's people to being more like Christ, closer to God, and greater ambassadors for the kingdom. Have a point for the things you are planning. If you're just picking songs because you like them, or the handbell choir is due for a performance because it's been a while and you a have worship set to fill, you're missing out on the fullness of having a God-breathed experience each week in store for your congregation. Know where you are going first, then lay the pavement to get there.

Sundays Come with Amazing Regularity

There's always a Sunday. There's always another one coming. Every. Single. Week. Sundays are relentless. That might ought to scare you. They will never cease, at least not until Jesus comes back. If I'm honest, there are times when it is daunting, if not overwhelming, that another Sunday is coming. When I'm sitting Monday morning in the office following up from all the little details and problems and conversations that arose from the previous Sunday, I almost feel myself need to take a huge swallow of air and let the reality settle for a minute that everything I did last week, I have to start it all over again. In our world as worship leaders, there's the added pressure of performance and if it wasn't a great week, doing it again can sometimes feel intimidating. Nevertheless, Sunday is coming. For me the relief comes in knowing that the new current week is already on track to be executed with excellence. Our church is ready for it, and I don't have to conjure it starting again on Monday morning. I *know* this because I rely on good tools for worship planning.

In particular, I'm talking using worship planning software. Now being as it's the twenty first century and maybe you're a millennial or a Gen Z you may be thinking "Is this even worth talking about"? Likely, you might be a leader already using something. However, my experience in a really transient part of the world where I get new volunteers all the time and most of them have never heard about what I'm about to talk about tells me there are still WAY too many churches out there not utilizing this resource. Let me be really blunt for a moment brothers and sisters in Christ; if you're not using one of the resources out there to help manage your ministry and plan your worship services, you need to put this book down and go sign up for one now. I'll be completely transparent in saying I'm a huge fan of Planning Center Online, and for my worship leading world in particular, their "Services" app is amazing. A decade ago, I jumped in to using the web-based service when it was, honestly, still in its infancy.

The very first week of using "Services" I saved myself *three* hours of work.

Three hours to devote to something else besides the nuts and bolts of planning worship. I used to spend my time creating endless Excel spreadsheets for orders of worship and schedules for team members. I built whole websites dedicated to posting these spreadsheets as well as music resources like chord charts and audio files for our worship ministry volunteers. Me, all by myself, alone. Hours and hours spent working on all of these needed tasks. Planning Center revolutionized my ministry, and their constant innovations and feature updates continue to do so about once a year. The other thing it gives me is unrivaled collaboration. My current ministry is substantial in size, and I have the luxury of delegating tasks like scheduling, CCLI reporting, and weekly song selections and this is only made possible because we utilize this wonderful cloud-based tool that allows many individuals to take part in the regular ongoing tasks necessary to conduct our ministry week in and week out.

There are several of these services out there and while I'm unapologetically a fan of one, you should be using *something*. There is a financial cost associated with it to be sure. I will be first in line to tell you it is worth the investment. You are a specialist in what you do and Lord willing you are paid well for what you do. Let me encourage you to have the same mentality towards a company that specializes in what they do, and that's making life easier for us worship leaders and church organizations through incredible software and technology.

You will undoubtedly find you have more available time to devote to other ministry matters. You should see that your ability to plan further ahead becomes easier. You'll feel more comfortable offloading tasks to members of your team because you can still maintain oversight and see that things are getting done in an efficient manner or be able to follow up when they're not. You should also feel your church staff is more cohesive because it allows for better communication with regards to upcoming events and content. Most importantly, Mondays won't seem so daunting with yet another Sunday staring you down without a long thought-out plan in place. I cannot stress enough how important it is to be utilizing one of the available resources to help manage your ministry and worship planning. And if you're having a hard time selling your church leadership on the need of the expense, have them contact me and I'll personally go to bat for you, I feel that strongly about it.

To Focus, Or NOT To Focus

In my years in ministry, I've been fortunate to attend a number of worship focused and worship leader centric conferences. They are always a great opportunity to refresh one's spirit with other believers who find themselves in the same ministry as me. There's always something to learn and worship is always phenomenal because there are several hundred worship leaders and musicians worshipping together. Most of these conferences offer breakout sessions to hear from other worship leaders on various topics ranging from anything such as vocal technique or A/V demonstrations. One session I almost always see offered is Worship Planning or something to that effect, and almost always the discussion centers around strategies for planning worship services that "focus" on a single message for each and every service a church might have. In other words, taking a single topic and making every element in a worship service all about that one single topic.

Let me be completely transparent here and say that everything that follows is my opinion and not based on any fundamental spiritual tenant. You can take it or leave it or drop me a line sometime and debate with me if you'd like to and tell me that I'm wrong, or that I'm right. However, my opinion is mine and I hold it firmly.

I think the concept of singular focused worship planning hardly plays out as intended in the real world.

Now, my opinion *is* based on over 25 years of planning and leading worship services in multiple styles at many different types of churches. Folks, I've tried this approach. I tried it a lot for many years. Let me explain my feelings and then hopefully you can form or alter your own opinion.

Having sat through those sessions at worship conferences, the concept sounds really great! It honestly sounds really spiritual and comes across as an effective, proactive strategy. It is really easy to hear the concepts of planning song selections, videos, dramas, and messages all around a singular concept and be convinced of this idea that worship planned in this manner will soar and every service will be one for the history books.

The real world plays out differently, or at least in my experience it has. For me, the concept impacts worship services negatively in two ways. The first is that it makes the experience become flat, or one-dimensional. Do you remember the salami and anchovy sandwich analogy I threw at you during the music selection chapter? For me, it's the same thing only instead of doing it with style choices, you're now doing it with theological concepts.

Imagine in your mind your pastor is teaching on grace one week. So, in the effort to focus the service on the topic, you make the song selections "Amazing Grace", "Your Grace is Enough", "Grace Like Rain", and "This Is Amazing Grace". You also choose a video mini-movie on grace, and the children's mini-message is also on God's grace. Ok, sure you've talked about grace and covered it in depth and for the lost/seekers they hear a message that impacts them immensely and one they needed desperately. But let's say I am an 85-year-old founding member of your church who's walked with the Lord my whole life and I understand I've been given grace. In fact, I understood it 75 years ago! I'm probably in a season of life where I'm more concerned with generational discipleship, generosity, legacy, sanctification, submission to lordship, or spiritual gifts. I've left the service at the end of the day probably disconnected and frustrated because my church was irrelevant to me due to the focus on a single topic.

In my experience, services where we have focused this narrowly in worship don't have the effect we were looking for. Instead of a tightly wrapped message that blows the lid off the building with response from our people, in the real world, people just honestly seem bored and disconnected because they've tuned out the "clanging cymbal" that is the day's focused message. It is honestly sad to see all that planning play out that way, but truthfully dear friend, I've seen it happen way too many times for me to feel positive about the approach.

The other way services are negatively impacted by the intense focus approach is that we restrict the movement of the Holy Spirit among our people. In other words, we're putting Him in a box.

Even if there are only ten people in your worship service, they are all different. They all have a different heritage, a different spiritual upbringing, a different course of their week, even a different morning drive in to church that day. This means they all need the Holy Spirit to minister to them differently in the midst of corporate worship and speak to them at different points along the walk with Christ. This reality only scales up as more people attend your service experience. Are you serving in a church of 100? 500? 6000? Do you think 6000 people all need the same laser focus? Let me strongly suggest that they don't. Again, this is my opinion, but one based on years of planning, executing, and experiencing hundreds, if not thousands of worship services.

Instead, my preferred approach is what I call "tee it up". Obviously, we want to be ordered in worship, we're biblically called to be. When we fail to provide structure and a plan for worship, we run the risk planning services worship experiences that look more like the inside of the scattered mind of a person with ADHD. So I'm *not* advocating for no focus. What I have found to be the more effective strategy is to keep the majority of content in a worship experience in the same ballpark as the message, but loosely connected, and leading to an apex. If the message is on grace, maybe include a song that talks God's justice and mercy being in balance. Then, when the moment is right in the service, we'll "tee up" pastor's message by hitting the piece of content in the worship set specifically on grace. A good worship planner will be diligent in thinking through connecting the dots that leads to teeing up the message. Then when the pastor steps on the platform to teach, hearts are dialed in to receive the meat of the day's message and not tuned out and your pastor is poised to "knock it out of the park".
I know…sports analogies, but you get the idea.

Teeing up the message dials in people's hearts and minds to what you really want people to hear for the service but not in a way the leaves some people bored, or others disenfranchised. Then the message of the day can build off a song, skit, or video that you specifically call attention to. My personal experience has shown this system has a greater impact on attendees because worship hasn't been watered down by the entire service's content. This process will honestly force you to be more creative in your worship planning because you'll have to be *more* intentional with your handoffs from moment to moment throughout the service. You'll be building roadmaps each week for worship. But, if done with prayer and good brainstorming, you should find your results to be healthy for your church congregation. You'll experience greater engagement in the midst of your service, greater retention of the point of the service, and greater appreciation for the dialed in content you do offer. I challenge you to intentionally try this approach for several weeks and evaluate the results. I'm willing to suggest you'll be pleased.

Worship is Like Food, Keep It Fresh

Very recently I took a trip across the United States to San Fransisco to visit some very close friends. We had an absolute blast doing touristy stuff all over the city. We happened to be there during the Cherry Blossom Festival which is held each year in Japan Town in the city. It's a beautiful festival filled will all kinds of traditional Japanese culture, activities, and there's even a parade. We had a great day. My wife and I were then supposed to travel home the next day. We went to bed early to catch an early flight in the morning.

Something poisoned me.

I woke up in the middle of the night and instantly knew something terrible was happening throughout my body. I felt like I was dying that night. I was ready to die because I felt so bad. I was ready to meet my savior on the other side. I wanted out so bad. We didn't make our flight the next morning. In fact, it took me another three days just to be able to be upright for more than an hour. With no exaggeration I can say it was the worst case of food poisoning I have ever experienced. And when I say poisoned, I can now vouch for why it is called food *poisoning.*

Something I had consumed that day at the festival (which was only sealed, packaged food by the way) had me as deathly sick as I have ever been in my life. I have no desire to ever revisit and eat there ever again as you can imagine.

Have you ever considered you might be poisoning your church by feeding it old, out of date food? Is your worship planning like a past date jug of milk? Or maybe your planning practices are a piece of chicken that's been sitting out at room temperature for way too long.

Are you repulsed yet? Do you want out yet?

Or at best, maybe your services are just stale, and stale isn't appealing. Maybe it's not repulsive, but it just isn't a positive experience.

Worship is like food, it should be kept fresh. "Variety is the spice of life." This is true for our worship services and how and what we plan. This is true for content for sure, but my point here is more service order and formatting.

I love salsa. There are few things I love as much as fresh, cold, really flavorful salsa. In fact, I've usually made up my mind about a new Mexican restaurant after sampling the salsa. And I'm not alone in this. Visit any Mexican restaurant and look around and see just how many people are chowing down on the stuff. Conversation at some point usually turns to the quality of the salsa. Salsa is a mix of a bunch of different ingredients but almost no two restaurants taste the same. Some are sweet, some are super hot. The variety is part of the appeal of the food.

If you have a hand in planning worship, a priority should always be keeping things fresh and vibrant. If you are leading the exact same service format each week, you can do better. Give your church some salsa. Mix things up, add different ingredients. Move elements around occasionally. Move the message to a different point in service. Lead a worship song at the end…or don't if you already always do. Hold a small group session in the midst of service. Move the equipment on your platform around; do it regularly. We move equipment and people every week! When people know what to expect they become complacent. Keeping things fluid maintains interest and buzz. Don't let your experiences become stale through monotony.

Think about what ministries around your church could contribute to your services. If you're serving in a traditional church setting, you might have an easier time with this. If your church has a choir, an orchestra, a handbell choir, a youth choir, a children's choir, a senior adult choir, and a deaf ministry, variety will likely fall in your lap. Those of us in contemporary settings with just a worship team/band, you're going to have to really flex the creative muscles. Maybe you don't have a children's choir but maybe you could recruit the kid's ministry to join your worship team for a song one week. Maybe you have a week where your small group leaders publicly celebrate what's happening in their groups. Our church holds a "Thankful Sunday" once a year and have various ministry leaders give reports on what God is doing through the work of our local church and that service doesn't look like anything else we do the rest of the year. Or maybe try working out with another local church a worship team swap for a week.

In the end, feed your congregation something new and fresh all the time. It's not good enough to every week do the same three song set, message time, and close with a reprise. You can certainly use that format, but it should be part of the salsa of what you plan. You might need to even be systematic about having a few base formats and decide on what percentage you'll use each format over the course of a year.

No matter what, don't force feed your church a steady diet of stale, rotten, or poisoned food week in and week out as you plan worship for your church. Keep them engaged by constantly providing something new that shakes them from complacency and monotony.

Refuse to Worship Plan Alone

As we discussed earlier, you should not be selecting music as just one person. The same is true for actually selecting content for individual worship services. You should engineer systems into your ministry where you plan worship services with a team, even if it's only a small team of crucial ministry leaders.

In my years, the times I have been closest to "ministry burn out" have been directly tied to lack of involving myself with other people in worship planning. When I have allowed myself to be on an island while choosing music, videos, guest speakers or dramas, those are the times when I have been the most depleted spiritually. Not only is it draining to constantly do all the work on *any* given project, but you once again put yourself in being in a position of being the lid of creativity and being the boundary of the movements of the Holy Spirit. Now I will say, it happens, a given Sunday is coming and the work needs to be done and you're in charge, so you do it. We've all been there. But you should be more systematic in planning ahead, and how you ensure other leaders in your church are a part of the process of mapping out your service and engineering the "tee up" for the week.

Where I serve, we have two services every Sunday and this translates to a lot of down time off the platform as a worship team. While we insist that our team members sit during one of our services and listen to the day's message with message notes in hand, there is lots of other time where our team is present that we can utilize. In some seasons, we make song selections for two to three weeks in advance during our first service of the day. Those that are able, we all gather in our Green Room and go over upcoming weeks and select appropriate music based on our message calendar, and we select (in pencil) who will be the Tier 3 vocalist to lead those particular selections on those Sundays. I seldom am the one who even has to facilitate these sessions anymore. Our band members and vocalists jump in and at this point it is so engrained in our team culture, this aspect takes place and I simply review choices later in the week.

At other times we have had specific meetings to plan. This is especially true for major events such as holiday programs or for activities such as vacation Bible schools or special worship nights. Regardless, I hardly plan anything myself anymore and my team largely handles the duties week in and week out. This allows me so much extra time to focus on other larger scale projects and planning.

The other really pleasing aspect about this kind of team involvement is that when, on the rare occasion, I tell my team I feel led to plan something and hold something close to my chest either because I have some creative idea or because there are some specific details that need to be worked out by the staff, my team understands there's a greater weight to my involvement and affords me great deference and respect in these moments. They trust that I have my reasons for needing to be the one to plan an event because I've earned so much credibility with my team. Trusting them builds trust in me among the team because of how much I have sought their involvement and skin in the game along the way. They know I'm not planning services because I want them to go a certain way out of my own selfish desires because I have demonstrated the norm is *not* for me to act that way.

By refusing to worship plan alone, our services are consistently a reflection of what God is speaking to our people. Our team approach allows for greater levels of creativity and sensitivity to the Holy Spirit and to His people. There are services that were amazing to witness and be a part of that I would have never been able to envision on my own. I'm creative, but nobody is that creative. And I'm in tune with my people, but at best a few at a time, certainly not my whole church. I'd be deceiving myself to think otherwise. I can't recommend enough that you begin to look around you and determine who could you involve in your worship planning process. You might only be able to start small with just one other person but do it. And determine your system for when and how often you are going to gather with your people to plan. This needs to be scheduled and on everyone's calendar. This needs to be a regular part of your ministry's flow week in and week out to ensure you never devolve to planning by yourself habitually.

Unleash your church's potential for really incredible and engaging worship experiences by minimizing how much of it you are responsible for. Your seasoning should be a part of the mix for sure, but you should move to a place where you are not the lone ingredient. Sundays come with amazing regularity, plan alone at your own risk. Do it for long enough and you'll find your services to be stale and predictable and you'll eventually succumb to the grind of constantly having to produce, and ministry burnout will quickly follow after that. For your church's good, and your own well-being, refuse to plan alone.

12 – Technical Difficulties

To acquire wisdom is to love yourself;
people who cherish understanding will prosper.

Proverbs 19:8

Technology is great…until it isn't.

When I answered the call to ministry, I couldn't wait for my days to be filled with troubleshooting computers, DMX programming, and replacing lamps for finicky projectors.

Please hear the facetious tone of my words.

As far as my story goes, no one told me how much of my time and mental capacity would be consumed with dealing with technology and not focused on "worship". To be clear, we don't need technology in worship. We absolutely *can* praise the God of the universe without a single watt of electricity. Praise and worship only require of us that our hearts be turned towards Him in adoration. Everything else after that is embellishment. And yet if your ministry is anything like mine, the 21st century has made its mark on our worship experiences. This is the norm of most churches in the developed world in the west, which I fully anticipate is the bulk of my audience for this book. That being true, more than likely it falls to the worship pastor or worship leader to oversee the church's use of technology in worship. You may find yourself in a church that can support having staff to work in this field for your church, and that undoubtedly will make your life easier on this front, but seeing as you likely oversee the overall experience of your service, you'll likely oversee these staff members as well. Whatever your situation, technology is a major component of the nuts and bolts of the "stuff" of our worship ministries these days. As such, you should be prepared to be the leading authority on the technology your ministry uses to help guide your church and your ministry in its implementation. Let's discuss some key aspects of your leadership of this critical aspect of your ministry.

Learn, Learn, and Learn Some More

L. R. Baggs Acoustic Preamp Pickup — quarter inch audio cable — Roland guitar digital effects processor — quarter inch audio cable — Digitech multi effects stomp box pedal — quarter inch audio cable — Direct input box — XLR audio cable — Allen and Heath Digital snake audio interface box — Cat5e Ethernet cable – Allen and Heath audio console.

The above sequence represents every piece of technology in my current setup just to get sound from my acoustic guitar to our sound board. And that doesn't consider the digital audio processing sequence to get sound out of the speakers in our worship auditorium. Add to that the rest of our worship team, all the audio, lights, projection of motion backgrounds and lyrics, robotic cameras, live video in the room and online, Wi-Fi network, click track and backing tracks, and the tech we use for charts for our musicians. And I'm more than likely forgetting more.

It's. A. Lot.

Your church might not be this complex. Then again, your church is very possibly more complex. I've been in environments more complicated and more cutting edge than my ministry for sure. One question I have for you is who knows how everything works in your church? Is there someone who has a complete grasp on what technology you're using and how it all interacts together? When it stops working, and it *will*, is there someone who can step in to solve the problem who knows what they're doing? Is there someone responsible for how *best* to use a piece of technology? I'm talking about implementation with excellence here! There should be someone! And I'm not talking about an outside A/V vendor, because let's be real, they're not going to show up Sunday morning when you're having a technology failure ten minutes before service. If your situation is like most churches I've experienced in my ministry career, it probably falls to the worship leader to be this person. And if you're one of the lucky few of us for whom it is not your direct responsibility, you have great capacity to have a major impact in this aspect of your church. Are you actually helpful or are you lacking in functional knowledge that could make you more of an asset? If it is important enough for you to utilize technology in your worship, for the health of your worship experience, I would assert that you need to be one of the leading experts on the tech you are using.

This means learning without ceasing. Learn, learn, and learn some more! Develop into your skills as a worship leader a hunger to learn. This applies to so many facets of our walk as believers obviously. As the saying goes "Leaders are learners." But I bring this point up specifically about technology because of the pace at which technology advances in our day and age. God's Word and His message are unchanging and so we can spend our entire lives devoted to scripture study, but the pace here is one of a constant steady growth, a slow burn even (but hopefully with passionate zeal). In contrast, technical knowledge these days rips at a blinding pace. I'm finding in a number of tech areas, "cutting edge" turns into "obsolete" in a matter of months!

For me the use of technology is a pursuit of staying relevant to modern church attendees. We use these tools not because we have to, but because we want to reach and speak to people in ways that capture their attention in a culture that is literally bathed in technology twenty-four hours a day, seven days a week. We literally wear it to bed at night so it can track our sleep patterns, heart rates, and oxygen levels. People are attuned to technology and its impact on our daily lives and to step into any gathering with no tech, or obsolete tech can make your environment feel dated and out of touch at best, or jarring at worst, for our modern congregants. We want welcoming inclusive environments and so we use the best tools we can to achieve that environment in the hopes of capturing hearts and minds for the cause for Christ. And so, we meet people where they are at, which includes a strong dose of the latest and greatest technology has to offer.

But the "latest and greatest" is a moving target, it is not fixed, so it is imperative that we must be always seeking to be educated on the tools we are using. This will take laser-focused intentionality on your part. There is no way this happens by accident. Leading through technology requires constant reading of training materials, websites, databases, and discussion boards. It requires consistent training from trusted sources. It requires picking the brains of others who have successfully implemented some piece of new tech into their corporate gathering experience. It requires attending conferences and seminars specifically centered around technology, its use, its trends, and what's coming around the corner with new innovations. Staying in the know might also require the service of outside vendors to keep you knowledgeable. You may need to get connected with groups on social media platforms dedicated to these pursuits; and yes, they do exist and are hugely helpful.

Most importantly, this investment in study must be routine. Find ways to build some time into your weekly, monthly, and/or seasonal schedules for knowledge building with regards to tech. Make sure you are mapping out whether it's greater understanding of the tech you are currently using, or tech you are considering integrating into your systems. Make time for both. Maybe it looks like finding a resource that will send you an email once a week on technology innovations for you to read. Seasonally, I tend to try to allow myself time for at least a brief webinar on some topic each spring, usually after Easter season when my life is in a calmer, slower season with more room for margin. Hopefully, its more than just a webinar but the idea is I'm looking for something substantial that will teach me something I don't know. Occasionally it works out that I'm able to attend a worship leader conference for multiple days and these events usually have great breakout sessions on technology topics specifically centered around implementation in worship.

But we should always be learning. We have to. With all the technology we use at my church, it is crucial that I be able to lead and guide my teams as we use these tools and I feel its safe to assume you're in the same situation. My teams, largely volunteers, don't have the same time or focus to devote to being the experts, so it's up to us as overseers of worship to make sure all our systems are up to date, and being utilized by our teams in a manner that builds up our worship gatherings and not destroy them because we don't know what we're doing with our tools. And trust me the technology we use absolutely holds the power to melt down our worship services if misused.

Just like Uncle Ben told Spiderman, "With great power comes great responsibility."

Technology is a Tool, Without Proper Training It's a Workplace Hazard

Recently, a member of our worship team called me to inform me he had to miss rehearsal and as a result was not going to be able to serve for the coming Sunday's services. Usually, these types of notices come over text these days but his situation was heavier and he was asking for prayer as well. His reason for missing, he informed me, involved an accident at his job. This worship team member worked at a manufacturing plant in our part of the world for a major tire manufacturing company. He told me that a colleague of his had unfortunately been injured as a result of not following protocol for a piece of machinery and the man had lost his arm in the mishap. The unfortunate accident had not only been tragic for the poor employee but had also caused a major shutdown and disruption to the plant and my worship team member was having to deal with the aftermath of the situation. He was going to be working extra to get the plant back up and running.

To my knowledge, no one has lost a limb in the midst of a worship service that I was leading. Thank the Lord!

But technology has managed to derail more than a few worship services in my time and burn several down completely more times than I'd like to admit. At the very least, moments have occurred where the distraction caused by some piece of tech becoming problematic is simply too much for a congregant to not tune out over our pastor's preaching and focus on something going wrong; which is simply heart breaking. Too much preparation on our part as the worship team and on our pastor's part for his message has transpired for me to ever be ok with these moments occurring.

A common thread in many of the cases of something going wrong has been a member our production team didn't have a good enough grasp of what their tech was capable of or hadn't had enough practice/prep time to ensure they didn't do something we didn't plan or practice. Now, please hear my heart in that I'm not blaming anyone in this or trying to shift culpability. If the blame falls anywhere, it falls on me as the leader and the overseer of the experience. And there are plenty of times when some piece of tech goes completely haywire and does whatever it wants. But the point stands that a significant number of the disruptions to our worship services caused by technology are a result of improper or missing training or improper execution.

To be a lead worshipper who uses technology requires that we take production team training very seriously. It doesn't matter at all if you have fully paid staff or have a production team entirely composed of volunteers; they need adequate and frequent training in the tech they are expected to use. Training needs to be intentional, strategic, repeatable, and scheduled regularly. Training begins with new recruits onboarding and never ends even for our seasoned veterans. If there is one thing I have learned through my years is that my team members never have as much knowledge as I assume them to. There is always something for us all to learn. There's always something more we could be doing better. There's always another piece of tech that might make what we're hoping to accomplish through technology better. We only build all this knowledge and experience into our team through training.

For my ministry, we train everybody no matter how long someone has served with us, or how much experience someone has before they come to us. The reason is our training also includes how we want things to be done. Sure, someone has twenty years of sound experience, but do they know the ins and outs of your specific operating procedures? Sure, they have served with your ministry for ten years, but do they recall the best practices they were taught to carry out five years ago? We train every moment we have time together in our space and outside that time as well. We train people at rehearsals; in fact, this is where most of our training occurs. Let me caution you not to rely on Sunday mornings for the bulk of your training time. There are too many moving parts, and the goal of the morning is too important for too many distractions that arise from getting someone trained in the midst of services. But we do train on Sunday mornings "on the job". It's hard to get a better feel for the importance of transitions and minimizing distractions than in the actual worship environment. We also train at special training sessions that we hold periodically where we can just focus as a production team without having platform team members around making all those "more reverb" demands. When we troubleshoot, we do so as a team so those who don't have the knowledge yet can learn best practices for problem solving. We send educational materials out to team members as homework to sharpen skills.

Our training looks like this process:
+ Shadowing
+ "Side by Side" Training
+ "Back Pocket" Training
+ A Solo Flight

Shadowing is exactly what it sounds like. We allow folks a week or two to just observe what we do and how we do it. This gives new recruits the opportunity to learn and decide which role(s) they want to train in. "Side by Side" training is the next step where we pair a trainer with a trainee and they work together to prepare for Sunday and the trainer is explaining the process and best practices as they go, allowing the trainee to do as much of the hands-on work as possible along the way. After that, "Back Pocket" training still includes a trainer, but the trainee is doing almost all the work with the trainer in that person's back pocket in case they come across something they can't remember or haven't learned yet. All of this takes around three to four weeks for a trainee to work through. The last step is for someone to run a position solo to validate their proficiency in the role. This is their "Solo Flight". Help is never far away, but they are running a position on their own.

We also don't guess *when* someone is trained. A trainee has to go through these weeks of training and completion has to be approved by their trainer(s), our Production Director, and by the trainee. Yes, the *trainee* has to approve they are ready. Remember my father-in-law? Had someone taken a moment to ask him if he felt ready or comfortable, he would have decidedly answered no. We never want to set someone free in a role if they themselves don't feel comfortable. You must include your trainees in this final approval conversation. If all three parties agree they are trained fully, then they are deemed "qualified" for that role and added to our schedule for that particular position. During this whole time, we are checking in with the trainees to encourage them and make sure they are feeling more comfortable with their role.

We're also providing reading materials to help them learn best practices for their role and our policies and procedures for how their individual position is expected to operate at our church. Let me encourage you to put all of these things on paper (or digital) for your people. Instead of guessing, decide how you want things to be done and provide that resource for your people. If you want ProPresenter prepared in a certain way every week, don't expect your people to be mind readers. Write it out and provide it to your team. If you want the sound mixed a certain way or at an average of a certain decibel reading, communicate it clearly and often.

Tracking of your training system is hugely crucial as well. We keep records (our records looks like a white board in our production booth) of who is currently trained in a specific role in the team, who is *currently* training, and who is cable of training others. We also insist that someone is only learning one position at a time. You may have that eager beaver who wants to do everything. Let me caution you against allowing someone to do this. For someone to be really proficient in a role it takes time and consistency. This simply doesn't happen when someone is bouncing between multiple roles. We find they simply don't retain the information we want them to in order to perform well in a given role. Once someone has become proficient in a role, however, we do insist on cross-training on our team. If you're a sound engineer, we want to know how to run lights as well. If you're a camera operator, we want you to know how to run lyric slides. You never know when someone will get sick or simply not show for a host of reasons, and you want someone to be able to adjust and slide into a crucial role and know what they're doing. Think of it as Production Team insurance. People certainly specialize in a given area of Production, but cross knowledge ensures that even when a team member has to miss at the last minute, someone else can step in and provide coverage. This is matter of team culture really. You as leader will have to work diligently to make sure no one feels like they "own" a role or are pigeonholed into a single role. Everyone being able to operate in multiple positions fosters the health of your Production Team by not being overly dependent on a single person for a particular job.

We can pull off some really cool things in the 21st century church. We can also become overly dependent on technology and when it melts down it's a workplace hazard for you with the capacity to destroy all your hard work in a single moment and unravel a worship service. Insist that your team take seriously the power they wield and devote themselves to running production with excellence. Excellence in this aspect of your ministry requires constant training and preparation with the tools you have to work with as a church.

Budget & Save For Technology Ahead of Time

In case you missed the memo, tech is expensive! I don't know about your church, but in my church, it is one of the big expense line items only beaten by payroll, missions, and building maintenance. In an effort to not have this book dated, I'm not going to get into specific costs and expenses, but I feel fairly safe in saying that cutting edge tech that is on the leading edge is always going to be a stretch for ministries to afford.

On top of that, stuff breaks, always, at the worst times.

My church has been struck by lightning three times in my tenure here. Insurance is a wonderful thing and has helped tremendously but replacing tech when it fails also usually means replacing it with something current (not an exact match to the old gear) and there's always costs even if it's just an insurance deductible.

If you're running a lot of tech at your church the time is now to pay for what's coming. Whatever influence you have over your church's budget planning you should be planning for technology expenses. Build in what you're going to need for the current year. But also the need budgeting for capital reserves for future investments is absolutely critical. If you can build capital reserves into your budget line items, it needs to be specific to technology and/or A/V. A number of churches I have known have the budget line lumped into general reserves or facilities maintenance but what I have witnessed with the extreme costs of technology is that leads to conflict over resources in the church. It also leads to flat inactivity on replacing outdated or failing gear. When there isn't a dedicated fund for technological needs, there's always going to be some other priority like an HVAC unit that goes out or similar repairs. Eventually this leads to a church failing to replace gear that directly impacts the church's major weekly worship experience and negatively impacts attendees' perception of the experience. When there are dedicated funds, it places a higher priority on the maintenance and upgrading of technology used and keeping the worship environment polished and up to date.

Planning should also be considered on lifespans for technology. Some gear can last a decade. Some gear might last six months if you're lucky. Some gear like projectors need regular lamp replacements that can be costly and occurs at regular intervals over the lifespan of the equipment. Your budgeting should include plans for all tech that will need replacing and the time intervals anticipated. Even if you don't make budgeting decisions at your church, this is a resource you could provide to those that do so they can make educated choices about allocating funds.

The alternative to planning your maintenance and upgrade costs ahead of time for your budget is you will constantly be scrambling when gear fails and fighting an uphill battle when something needs to be upgraded simply because it's out of date. If it works, it's not broken, right? You and I know that's not always right but that's the perception, especially in churches where resources are always seen as limited. As always, be a good steward of the resources you have to work with but part of the use of technology means keeping tech in good working order and not so obsolete it becomes a constant distraction rather than useful tool to lift high the glory of God in worship.

The Biggest Mistake You'll Make (Until Now)

YAY! You did it! You pulled it off and it's awesome! You finally got that huge upgrade done. That flashy, horribly expensive thing you've been dreaming about for a couple years and begging your church leadership for, it is finally here. It's installed, up and running, and it's everything you've been dreaming about and more.

Twenty years later... your dream is the next administration's nightmare.

I'll state it very simply, the biggest mistake you'll make with technology is falling into the trap of thinking that once you're done, you're done. Once a major repair or upgrade is accomplished, far too many churches in my experience fall into the trap of thinking that's it. It's done. I have physically sat through church leadership teams where there is palpable shock at a needed expense because in the minds of everyone else, that piece of tech was 'just purchased" or "recently upgraded". Almost always 'just" or "recently" turns out to be at least five years. Friends of mine in other ministries have had similar conversations over technology that's over twenty years old! Twenty years ago from the writing of this book, the iPhone didn't exist yet. Imagine the gear they were talking about upgrading.

The reality, friends, is that churches get stuck. This happens to ministries as a whole. What once worked and was cutting edge gets old, worn out, and obsolete. The pace of technological advancements only makes this worse for the church production world.

You have to keep a mindset, and help your church keep a mindset, that investments in technology are temporal. Every piece of gear has a ticking clock. Yes, stuff breaks, but I'm talking about usefulness. There are times we as the church allow ourselves to be handcuffed by bad technology simply because we already own it. And so, it stays in place far beyond when it really should.

A friend of mine was tasked with setting up the capability to stream on social media for a church he recently got hired at as Production Director. He soon discovered the internet network had been installed about ten years prior. The age of the gear meant its max speed capacity was 100Mbps, which if you know anything about trying to stream video, 100Mbps is a huge impediment. He reported back to his superiors the situation and the cost of almost $20K needed just to upgrade the campus's network infrastructure before even considering the cost of video equipment. Suddenly a simple hardware upgrade became a major dispute among staff about whether to move forward and where the funds would come from (they didn't have a plan built into their budget for future tech upgrades!). No one along the way had minded the internet network and kept up with incremental improvements which led to this major impasse for the church and the situation held them back from a trend in ministry of being able to share the gospel online via social media.

If we are going to include technology in our worship space, and also our working space, we must give the very best to God. If a sound system is operational but is twenty-five years old and is harsh and unpleasant to listen to because the cones are slap wore out, they're likely turning people off from your experience. Attendees don't come back to your service when their ears hurt. You want to be streaming on social media but you're working with an analog audio console with no digital processing, I promise your online presence is not going to be what you think or pray that it is. It becomes a destructive force to your worship experiences rather than a useful tool to envelop people in an environment where they can commune with God free from distraction.

Your dance with technology is never over. Always keep pursuing improvement. We are called to offer our best with excellence in worship, remember? This applies to your technology also. Do the work of keeping your production resources up to date and pleasant to experience and a blessing to your church. And certainly, don't leave a degraded obsolete mess for whoever comes behind you some day. Keep the tools sharp and useful to bless your worship experiences and those who will pick up the tool bag sometime after you have moved on so they can do the same.

As I'm writing this my lead pastor's wireless headset mic just dopped out of signal in service! See, there's always something with technology. Stay on top of it. Gotta go!

FINAL THOUGHTS

13 – Crave the Worship Leader You Will Become Tomorrow

Rather, you must grow in the grace and knowledge of our Lord and Savior Jesus Christ.

All glory to him, both now and forever! Amen.

2 Peter 3:18 NLT

Whether you're just starting out in worship ministry, or you have been running this race for a long time, you have a lot of work to do. Sundays come around with amazing regularity and ministry is messy, filled with wonderfully messy people who aways make the work of the Lord more complicated. If you haven't buried your ego yet, let me tell you there is only so much of you to go around and only so skilled and talented that you're going to be. To last as a lead worshipper, you must crave the worship leader God intends for you to be. Crave who God will mold you to be. But remember this…

Let God do the work.

And by let God do the work I mean let God do a work *in* you. Daily submit to being his servant leader. Allow his Holy Spirit to speak and work through you and don't rely on your own strength to conjure everything you're going to need to have a lasting fruitful ministry. Live every moment of every day as your example of worship to other believers, the world, and to your worship team (Romans 12:1-2). You simply don't have enough energy, creativity, patience, or steadfastness to be enough. Let God be enough. Let Him guide you in all your decisions. Pray for His wisdom daily as you lead and guide musicians, techies, dancers, choir members, children, teens, seniors, believers, and unbelievers.

And never give up on the pursuit of knowledge. Stay in His word and hide His word in your heart. Study as often as your life allows. Study scripture. Study theology. Study worship theology. Study other ministries and their successes and failures. Study colleagues and the tidbits of knowledge they have learned. Study artists and creatives. Knowledge is the bedrock of wisdom, but knowledge alone is not enough. Wisdom is using good knowledge through His leadership for the uplifting of God's people or advancing His kingdom. But in your study and pursuit of wisdom, remember to be who God has made your to be.

Emulate, don't copy.

There are a number of flashy, successful, popular churches and ministries out there and the temptation will be to copy what looks like it's working somewhere else. There are flashy worship leaders and artists, too. Remember that it takes all kinds of churches to reach all kinds of people. Stand firm in the identity that God has given you in Christ and rest in where you are planted to serve and be determined to thrive as you work to have your church thrive. Borrow ideas and integrate them into your setting, learning from what others have learned the hard way, but tailor them to your voice and to the voice of your local church. Even my ideas, they work where I am, but they are going to need to adjust to your situation. Don't copy in black and white. Color in the spaces of ministry with the vibrancy of *your* personality, *your* ministry, *your* team, and *your* church.

My prayer is sincerely that there is something you found in these pages that will help you personally, help you professionally, or help your ministry or church. It has been my goal to give you something I wasn't given; a great resource to make my team better. I pray this book is part of the grander story that is your success as lead worshipper.

Know that God has *chosen* you to be the lead worshipper; be encouraged that you are anointed for this time. God planned for you to be in this role and likewise prepared you for your season as worship leader, however long that may be. Rest in that knowledge and take comfort from knowing that throughout time He set this moment aside specifically for you. You got this, now go give it your all for His Kingdom.

I'll close with this. When I was a youth, I grew up in a church that had a fantastic youth choir. We cut a few albums through the years, and we toured for a week each summer, putting on concerts at churches or places of ministry like homeless shelters. In a lot of way that youth choir was our youth group. At each concert we performed, we would always close the same way performing John Rutter's arrangement of the prayer blessing found in Numbers 6:24-26 (New Living Translation, 1996/2015) titled "The Lord Bless You and Keep You". At the end of every tour at our homecoming concert we would always invite any previous tour alumni to join us for the song. It was a favorite of ours because of the beauty of the words, the music, and the community. It was our tradition each concert, each year, each tour, each homecoming. It was the way we put a bow on our huge accomplishment. It was how we honored those who had come before us and taught us the way. It was how we stayed focused on keeping ministry to others the central focus. It was how we treasured God's precious Word. It was how we used our art and performance to elevate all of these things in one really powerful, spiritual moment.

In that spirit, my prayer and hope for you is this:

> 24 "'The Lord bless you and keep you;
> 25 the Lord make his face shine on you
> and be gracious to you;
> 26 the Lord turn his face toward you
> and give you peace.'"

Amen.

Resource Websites

Planning Center
Loop Community
Worship Online
Praise Charts
Multitracks
ProPresenter
Igniter Media
Sweetwater

Software Recommendations

Planning Center Apps
       + Services
       + Music Stand
Loop Community Prime App for multitracks/loops
Ableton Live
Corel Video Studio
VMix
Reaper

Worship Team System Ideas

➤ Worship Arts Team Vocalist Development Strategy (Tier
   System)

In the pursuit of excellence in our worship services,
Liberty has adopted an intentional strategy for including,
developing, training, and scheduling of vocalists. This strategy
is designed to help singers thrive based on their talent level,
demonstrated commitment level, performance capacity, and

experience within the Worship Arts Team. Vocalists will be assigned to the following Tier system and worship planning and vocalist scheduling will be conducted with this strategy in mind.

Tier I

    Requisites

        O Initial WAT Audition Process

    Role

        O Tier I Vocalists serve as members of the Worship Choir

        O Function as a leading presence during worship services to inspire congregation members to engage in worship

        O All new WAT Vocalists will serve as Tier I regardless of talent or previous experience

    Requirements

        O Average-Good vocal technique including pitch, tone, and knowledge of music and song selections

        O Able to blend and collaborate well with other vocalists in a group

        O Aid in providing infectious presence in leading worship as part of total Worship Choir

Tier II

    Requisites

        O Serve a minimum of 3 months as Tier I

        O Demonstrate strong commitment to WAT as Tier I vocalist

            + Abiding by WAT Covenant

            + Attendance

            + Attitude

O Tier II Audition Process

O Approval from any two current Tier III Vocalists and Worship Pastor

Role

O Tier II Vocalists serve as Backing-Lead Vocalists on mics

O Continue to fulfill Role and Requirements of Tier I Vocalist including participating in Worship Choir

O Joyful and celebratory presence leading worship

Requirements

O Demonstrate Strong vocal technique including ability to carry main melodies solo and/or strong ability to harmonize

O Strong Practice and Preparation Habits

O Strong Knowledge of song flow

O Strong, leading platform presence and worship spirit/attitude

O Ability to lead small sections of songs vocally such as a single verse, chorus, or bridge

O Strong witness and character in and around Church and community at large

Tier III

Requisites

O Serve a minimum of 3 months as Tier II Vocalist

O Demonstrate strong commitment to WAT via attendance and attitude as Tier I and Tier II vocalist

O Tier III Audition Process

O Approval from any two current Tier III
Vocalists, one Production Director, and
Worship Arts Pastor

Role

O Serve as Lead vocalist on mics
O Serve as worship service main leader with
anointed and commanding presence
O Continue to fulfill Role and Requirements of
Tier I and Tier II vocalist

Requirements

O Demonstrate strong control of vocal
technique especially concerning pitch, tone, and
phrasing
O High level of practice and preparation habits
O Demonstrate strong knowledge of song flow,
song selection, and multiple vocal parts
O Demonstrate ability to lead song sections solo
as Tier II vocalist
O Strong leading platform presence and worship
spirit/attitude including ability to lead verbally
through verbal cues and prayer
O Strong witness and character in and around
church, other ministry engagement at church,
and involvement in the community at large

➢ WAT Weekly Task Checklist

WAT Weekly Checklist

	Week Date	Week Date	Week Date
1) Song Selections made In Planning Center			
2) Assign Singers / Move Tiers			
3) Make Click Track Setlist in LoopCommunity.com			
4) Download Prime Setlist to click iPad and make sure sound settings are on right settings (Merideth Andrews & Digital)			
5) Make ProPresenter Playlist			
6) Check for WorshipOnline Vocal Tracks			
7) Dinner Sign-Up and in Meal Train			
8) Confirm Team (On Monday) and drop Unconfirms (For Band & Vocals)			
9) Confirm Tech Team Fully Covered			
10) Vocal Cues Drawn in Music Stand (Trey)			
11) Assign Leadspots in Order of Worship Production Notes			
11) Print Order of Worship (On Wednesday before Rehearsal)			

➤ Song Prep Checklist

<u>**Song Prep CheckList**</u>

	Song 1	Song 2
1) See if there is click track available at all? See if there is Praise Charts?		
2) Go to YouTube and find song. Determine original key signature.		
3) Compare to click track and make sure click track is good and usable compared to original song. If a good match, purchase click track.		
4) Rip YouTube into mp3 format.		
5) Praise Charts – Convert to correct key signature if not already. Purchase. Edit Chords / Arrangement.		
6) Compare chord chart to click track and make chord chart match the descriptions being vocalized in click track.		
7) Check Worship Online for vocal tracks of song and pull any available into mp3. Use Video Download Helper - Chrome Extension		
8) Create new song in Planning Center.		
9) Name arrangement "Original Key - "_"" and delete any sequencing that came in from CCLI, as well as give it correct original key signature.		
10) Upload YouTube MP3, Worship Online Vocals, Chord Chart all into Default Arrangement.		
11) Tag as WAT / LSM / Christmas as needed.		

<u>WAYS TO LABEL FILES FOR UNIFORMITY:</u>
MP3:
- Name (Artist) - Key Signature
    - ex. Firm Foundation (The Belonging Co.) - Bb

Chord Chart WITH NO GUITAR VERSION:
- "Song Name" Chord Chart - Key Sig

Chord Chart WITH GUITAR VERSION:
- "Song Name" Chord Chart - Key Sig. - Bass. Keyboard Version
- "Song Name" Chord Chart - Key Sig. - Capo 1st Fret Guitar Version

Worship Online Files:
- Name - Key Sig. - Voice Part (Alto, Tenor, etc.) Vocal Mixdown
    - ex. Firm Foundation - Bb - Alto Vocal Mixdown

Reference

New Living Translation. (2015). New Living Translation.
    https://www.tyndale.com/nlt/ (Original work published
    1996)